Books are to be returned on or before
the last date below.

7 Day Loan

LIBREX—

This edition published in Great Britain in 2009 by

The Policy Press
University of Bristol
Fourth Floor
Beacon House
Queen's Road
Bristol BS8 1QU
UK

tel +44 (0)117 331 4054
fax +44 (0)117 331 4093
e-mail tpp-info@bristol.ac.uk
www.policypress.co.uk

North American office:
The Policy Press
c/o International Specialized Books Services
920 NE 58th Avenue, Suite 300
Portland, OR 97213-3786, USA
tel +1 503 287 3093
fax +1 503 280 8832
e-mail info@isbs.com

British Library Cataloguing in Publication Data
A catalogue record for this book is available from the British Library.

Library of Congress Cataloging-in-Publication Data
A catalog record for this book has been requested.

ISBN 978 1 84742 179 1 paperback
ISBN 978 1 84742 188 3 hardcover

Cover design by Qube Design Associates, Bristol
Front cover: image kindly supplied by Paul Green
Printed and bound in Great Britain by the MPG Books Group

Contents

Notes on contributors

Helen Connolly is a researcher and a PhD student at the University of Bedfordshire. Her thesis considers the ways in which unaccompanied young people living within the UK interpret the United Nations Convention on the Rights of the Child relative to their asylum and resettlement experiences. Helen has also researched and written about the lives of children in public care. With a combined interest in both child welfare practice and theory, her work has focused on the common ground between childcare settings, provisions and outcomes, as well as the relevance of resilience theory and identity theory to frontline childcare practice.

Sarah Judd is Research Officer for Research In Practice, a department of the Dartington Hall Trust run in collaboration with the University of Sheffield, the Association of Directors of Children's Services and a network of over 100 partner agencies in England and Wales. She deals with research questions sent in to the website and provides enquirers with relevant recent research on a specific topic. She develops and writes the Performance Pointer series of briefings, which aims to bring performance management and evidence-informed practice closer together. She acts as the Regional Lead for the West Midlands, and helps with the dissemination of research among teams in local authorities in this area. She also represents Research In Practice on the Children's Services Research Forum, a collection of national research organisations that meets to discuss the implementation of research messages into practice.

George Julian became the Assistant Director of Research in Practice *for Adults* in July 2009, having joined as a research and development officer in 2006. George leads on two Change Projects, one focusing on safeguarding adults and the other exploring the changing ways of working under self-directed support. Her previous experience includes the post of senior research officer for National Statistics, research assistant looking at early years provision for children with special needs in Ireland and lecturer in special education.

Ravi K.S. Kohli is Head of Applied Social Studies at the University of Bedfordshire. He qualified as a social worker in 1984. His research has primarily focused on the arrival and resettlement of unaccompanied asylum-seeking children and young people in the UK. He has written a number of books and articles on this subject, and is currently looking at the experiences of unaccompanied minors leaving foster care and the ways in which they find a new sense of home as they grow into adulthood.

Gillian MacIntyre is a lecturer in the Glasgow School of Social Work, University of Strathclyde. Her main research interests are in the areas of learning disability and mental health. She has worked on a range of research projects including the health needs of people with learning disabilities, and a three-year project funded by the Department of Health to evaluate the new social work degree in England. This project used the principle of realistic evaluation and adopted a variety of methods including stakeholder interviews, focus groups, a postal questionnaire, a telephone survey and a skills analysis using vignettes. Her PhD focused on transitions for young people with learning disabilities.

Alison Petch has spent most of her career researching a range of health and social policy issues. From 1985 to 1993, she worked in the Social Work Research Centre at the University of Stirling, and from 1993 to 2005, was Director of the Nuffield Centre for Community Care Studies at Glasgow University. Funded by the Nuffield Trust, the Centre had as its focus the evaluation, promotion and dissemination of community care policy and practice in a multidisciplinary and multiagency context. In October 2005, Alison moved to the Dartington Hall Trust as Director of Research in Practice *for Adults*, an organisation established to promote evidence-informed policy and practice across adult social care. Alison has acted as an adviser to inquiries for both the Westminster and Scottish Parliaments and was a member of the Care Development Group, which advised on the implementation of free personal care for older people in Scotland.

Mike Stein is a research professor in the Social Policy Research Unit at the University of York. During the last 28 years he has been researching the problems and challenges faced by young people leaving care. He has also researched the experiences of young people running away from home and care. His current research includes the maltreatment of adolescents. He is a coordinator of the International Research Group, Transitions to Adulthood for Young People Leaving Public Care, and has published extensively in the field (www.york.ac.uk/swrdu). He has been involved in the preparation of training materials, as well as guidance for leaving care legislation in the UK, and has also been consulted on the development of leaving care services internationally.

Acknowledgements

This volume emerged from one of the annual events organised jointly by Research In Practice and Research in Practice *for Adults*. Both organisations focus on the promotion of evidence-informed policy and practice in children's and adults' services respectively; they seek to act as the brokers of knowledge between researcher and practitioner. They are partnership organisations, providing a range of resources to their partner agencies. The theme of transitions provided the focus for the councillors' and trustees' seminar in 2006 and, prompted by the then adults' and children's directors from Essex, this led to the further exploration of the theme in this volume. We are indebted to Alison Shaw and her staff at The Policy Press for their encouragement and to our authors for developing our thinking further

ONE

Introduction

Alison Petch

Much has been written over the years about the change process and change management, how to survive and indeed thrive on transformation in service structures and philosophies. There has been less focus on the individual whose identity remains constant but who, as a result of the disjunctures in organisational structures, has to negotiate a series of transitions from one arena to another. Moreover, such transitions may be accompanied by uncertainties and a potential change of status may generate anxiety and distress. This volume explores a range of transitions that are commonly encountered by those likely to receive support from children's or adults' services. While some of these occur because of people moving across organisational boundaries, others are triggered as a result of decisions taken by individuals themselves. The aim is to promote policy and practice that can enable these transitions to be achieved with the most effective outcomes for the individuals concerned.

Transitions are of course a regular occurrence across an individual's lifetime. The majority of people move from childhood to adulthood and from education to work; many will move into relationships, parenting and grandparenting; will move in and out of the labour market; will experience ageing and possibly physical moves and transitions in health status associated with that stage. Many argue that transition should be considered as a process rather than as a single event, a period of adjustment and recalibration. Such an approach allows particular appreciation of the potential consequences of the unanticipated event, the sudden illness, death or disruption that may precipitate a period of crisis.

When the term 'transitions' is used in the context of social services, it is usually the stage of transition from child to adult and from children's to adults' services that first comes to mind. Particular attention is often focused on those for whom this may present additional challenges, for example young people with learning disabilities or mental health problems or children leaving the care system. However, transitions occur both throughout the stages of the life cycle and also within each stage and there are a range of other transitions that are of relevance to our target audience. These include transitions between different housing and support situations, for example older people moving into extra-care housing or care homes or individuals moving to more independent living situations; transitions in status, for example from asylum seeker to accepted resident; and transitions across different organisational structures, for example in and out of specialist teams. Threaded throughout these major events are what have been termed 'micro-transitions', for example a gradual loss of hearing, becoming less active, taking on the mantle of an unpaid carer.

This introductory chapter will discuss what is meant by 'transitions' in the context of the support of children and adults and will define the scope of the volume. It will introduce the key areas to be addressed, detailing the way in which they can be considered together as a coherent contribution to the situation of transition and to the challenges that it presents to practitioners. It will seek to alert practitioners and policy makers to common responses likely to be associated with transition, whether that be the result of a carefully planned pathway or the product of disruption.

An early model developed by Hopson and Adams (1976), which sought to explain how individuals respond to major transitions, remains relevant today. They suggest that individuals experience seven key stages in the course of a major transition:

(1) immobilisation (a sense of being frozen, unable to act or understand);
(2) minimisation (denial that change is important);
(3) depression;
(4) acceptance (realisation that there is no going back);
(5) testing (trying out new behaviours to cope with the situation);
(6) seeking meanings (reflecting on change);
(7) internalisation (the new meanings discovered become part of behaviour and a new identity).

Although this is perhaps overly weighted towards the more negative perspective, it is nonetheless important for appreciating that even if a particular transition is potentially welcomed, it will often trigger a period of uncertainty and doubt.

Different people will of course experience transitions in different ways and one of the skills of the practitioner is to be able to identify and respond to each individual's particular experience. One of the concepts that has gained increasing recognition in recent years is that of 'hardiness' or resilience, seeking to explain why one individual appears able to cope with stressful life events that for another individual would prove a major challenge. An early formulation by Pearlin and Schooler (1978) distinguished between coping *resources* and coping *responses*. The former refer to the toolkit the individual has available to them and can be divided into psychological and social resources. Psychological resources refer to attributes, such as commitment and a willingness to view change as a challenge rather than a threat, that can assist an individual to cope with the changes inherent in any transition. Social resources include the networks in which the individual is located. Coping responses refer to what the individual does in response to the transitional change. Accessing a social network for support, for example, may assist an individual to weather a transition that for another individual may be overwhelming. The impact of negative social and economic factors such as poverty, discrimination, unemployment and social exclusion on the ability to cope is also highlighted.

Two examples will perhaps illustrate this discussion. Elsey et al (2007) have reviewed the research on vulnerable young people and their transition to independent living. They highlight that for many young people from well-resourced families there is increasingly a period of 'extended dependency', the break from home and into an independent household being negotiated over several years. This provides a sharp contrast to the more rapid and challenging transition of those leaving care or moving from a family that lacks economic or social capital. Elsey et al characterise this transition for those from care in particular as being 'accelerated and compressed'. This contrast had also been identified by the Social Exclusion Unit (SEU, 2005) in its study of transitions for young adults with complex needs. It further extended the analysis to characterise 'yo-yo transitions', a pattern of reversible and fragmented transitions.

The second example also focuses on transitions for young people (Furlong et al, 2003). The authors develop a model of transition that seeks to take into account the individual processes of negotiation that take place within the structural constraints. Rather than seeing young people as obtaining or not obtaining employment on the basis of the current health of the labour market, they recognise the importance of rationalisation and negotiation by the individual – ' a deeper understanding of the relationship between external contexts, individual resources and processes of active life management' (Furlong et al, 2003, p 5). Such an approach takes into account both subjective and objective dimensions of an individual's situation and the ways in which the individual draws on the resources available. These are likely to include educational qualifications, vocational training and skills, and family resources. Deficits in one area of resources (for example qualifications) may be compensated for by others (for example family support). For some, the transition will take a simple linear form, for others it will be non-linear and more risky.

Examples such as this offer transferable opportunities for reflecting on their implications for the range of different situations in which transition takes place. Following a chapter on the organisational context (Chapter Two), this volume explores the challenges of transitions for four particular groups of young people: those leaving care, those with learning disabilities, those with mental health problems and those seeking asylum.

In Chapter Three, Mike Stein highlights the importance of understanding the transition for young people leaving care as part of their broader lifecourse, and, as prefaced above, as 'fast-track' compared to their peers in the wider community. Three main experiences of transition are identified: those who successfully move on, those who 'survive', often as a result of the personal and professional support they receive, and those for whom past experiences are already damaging and future life chances are poor.

As discussed by Gillian MacIntyre in Chapter Four, young people with learning disabilities are often, particularly vulnerable to the varying age limits and eligibility structures of different support services. They are also very much at the heart of changing expectations in terms of social inclusion, with the aspiration for exercising wider choices and accessing employment. The last in particular remains for many young people with learning disabilities an aspiration rather than a reality. The chapter poses important questions as to whether current priorities are necessarily the most appropriate: 'a more meaningful transition plan might focus on building and establishing meaningful relationships and community links rather than emphasising employment'.

In Chapter Five, Sarah Judd considers transition from the perspective of young people with mental health problems. This is of course a more fluid group than the two already identified in that the need for support will vary over time. Major disjunctures occur, however, at the boundary between children's and adults' mental health services, with continuing support often not available once young people become adult. The concept of transition has therefore to be broader, not necessarily moving on to further mental health service provision but to more holistic support from a range of sources.

The experiences of young people seeking asylum provide the focus for Chapter Six by Ravi Kohli and Helen Connolly. Their absorbing chapter frames transitions as 'the ways in which you make sense of what has happened to you'; for many there is little certainty for the future. Working within these constraints, they offer invaluable insights for those seeking to support these young people.

The remaining chapters in the volume are focused more on the adult world. In Chapter Seven, George Julian maps the radical changes currently seeking to transform adult social services – from service provision to self-directed support. She addresses in particular the perspective of the worker seeking to navigate and accommodate the transition to the new system and offers strategies for both embracing and promoting the new model. Case studies are then presented of two key areas (Chapters Eight and Nine).

As presented in Chapter Eight, the transition to supported living for older people can take a variety of forms, but particularly when it involves physical relocation it can invoke a wide range of conflicting responses. This chapter looks in particular at the transition to the care home and the transition to some form of continuing care community. The evidence base for different support arrangements is explored, and practical strategies for the most effective management of the transition are detailed.

The final case study, presented in Chapter Nine, focuses on hospital discharge, a transition that is both one of the most common but also one beset with enduring challenges. It highlights those elements that repeatedly emerge as problematic and suggests steps that can be taken to minimise the disruption for individuals.

The final chapter of the book (Chapter Ten) seeks to identify the common elements across these different situations and to detail a range of practical suggestions for ensuring that practice and policy support rather than inhibit the opportunities that periods of transition can present.

References

Elsey, S., Backett-Milburn, K. and Jamieson, L. (2007) *Review of research on vulnerable young people and their transition to independent living*, Edinburgh: Scottish Executive Research.

Furlong, A., Carmel, F., Biggart, A., Sweeting, H. and West, P. (2003) *Youth transitions: Patterns of vulnerability and processes of social inclusion*, Edinburgh: Scottish Executive Social Research.

Hopson, B. and Adams, J. (1976) 'Towards an understanding of transition', in J. Adams, B. Hopson and H. Hayes (eds) *Transition: Understanding and managing personal change*, London: Martin Robertson.

Pearlin, N.I. and Schooler, C. (1978) 'The structure of coping', *Journal of Health and Social Behaviour*, vol 19, pp 2-21.

SEU (Social Exclusion Unit) (2005) *Transitions: A Social Exclusion Unit final report on young adults with complex needs*, London: SEU.

TWO

The organisational context

Alison Petch

Introduction

The separation of social service organisations into separate departments for children and for adults has prompted much of the recent discussion around transition. While points of transition have always required careful management, this is even more the case now that the responsibility for individuals may move from one department to another. For example, the needs of young people with learning disabilities become the responsibility of a different department once they reach adulthood, with potentially different procedures and eligibilities. More widely, transitions for individuals may also require management of boundaries and partnership working between traditionally separate departments, for example housing and social services, health agencies and the voluntary sector, the benefits agency and training providers. This chapter will map the key organisational contexts that create many of the transition experiences. Statutory service configurations for social services and health across the constituent countries of the UK will be considered first, followed by other organisations commonly involved in transition.

England

Social services

The delivery of social services support in England is the responsibility of the 152 local authority councils with social services responsibilities. Traditionally, a single local authority department had responsibility for both children's and adults' services. The pursuit of the 2003 Every Child Matters agenda (DfES, 2003) and the 2004 Children Act, however, triggered a reconfiguration of the landscape, with an increasing separation of the services and the creation of two distinct directorates. The 2004 Act required all local authorities with responsibility for educational and social services to appoint a Director of Children's Services (DCS), with responsibility for coordinating and managing the provision of local children's services across education, health and social services. The creation of this new statutory post was designed to ensure a coordinated approach to meeting the needs of all children and young people in the wake of the shortcomings revealed by the Laming Report on the Victoria Climbié case (Lord Laming, 2003).

Detailed guidance was produced in 2005 on the role of the DCS and the associated Lead Member role (DCSF, 2005). A consultation on an updated version of this guidance has just closed at the time of writing (February 2009) (DCSF, 2008). This sets out the role of the DCS as follows:

> The Director of Children's Services is tasked with enabling all children and young people in the area to achieve their potential across all five outcomes and to ensure that the outcomes gaps between the most disadvantaged children and their peers are reduced. This can only be achieved through provision of excellent services in which the local authority and its partners in the Children's Trust work together focusing on the needs of the child, young person and family. (DCSF, 2008, para 3.1)

The broad remit of the role is emphasised:

> As a member of the local authority senior management team the DCS should contribute to planning the provision of the full range of council services and promote the interests of children, young people and families across the range of local authority services, including planning, housing, transport and leisure. (DCSF, 2008, para 3.7)

and the key roles are listed:

a) leadership:

- within the local authority to sustain the necessary changes to culture and practice;
- within the local authority's area, so that all services contribute to improving outcomes for all and narrowing the gap for disadvantaged groups;

b) championing children, young people and their families within the local area, in particular through:

- professional leadership of the Children's Trust and engagement with the Local Strategic Partnership by strengthening the Children's Trust (and wider Local Strategic Partnership) to sustain effective joint working with and between bodies which commission, provide, or have an interest in services affecting local children and young people;
- production and publication of the Children and Young People's Plan and the relevant targets within the Local Area Agreement (along with the statutory DCSF targets);

c) safeguarding children – promoting the safety and welfare of children across all agencies; especially looked after children; and

d) management of the local authority's children's services, with professional responsibility and accountability for their effectiveness, availability and value for money. (DCSF, 2008, para 3.14)

One of the key principles of the Every Child Matters programme was that all children's services in each area be closely linked together in a children's trust by April 2008 and be led by a local authority DCS. This means that local authority education and children's services departments should be working closely with children's health services, Connexions and Youth Offending Teams. There is also a core role in response to the Youth Crime Action Plan of July 2008. Implementation of the Plan will require cooperation across agencies, 'bridging the divide between the social welfare state and the criminal justice system so young people's wider needs are addressed and effective transitions occur' (DCSF, 2008, para 4.5).

The introduction of the post of Director of Adult Social Services (DASS) alongside the DCS was designed to ensure that all the social care needs of local communities be given equal emphasis and be managed in a coordinated way. Statutory and best practice guidance on the role of the DASS was published in May 2006 as part of the changes to Chief Officer portfolios in the wake of the 2004 Children Act 2004 (DH, 2006a, 2006b). At the consultation stage, a key issue of concern raised by stakeholders had been the need for parity in arrangements between the DASS and the DCS. The new guidance has addressed this by ensuring that the functions and responsibilities of the DASS are equivalent to those of the DCS. In addition, the guidance set out the Department of Health's intention to introduce legislation requiring the appointment of a Lead Member for Adult Services at the earliest opportunity.

The focus of the DASS role is on delivering the core elements of *Our health, our care, our say* (DH, 2006c):

- improving preventative services and delivering earlier intervention;
- managing the necessary cultural change to give people greater choice and control over services;
- tackling inequalities and improving access to services;
- increasing support for people with the highest levels of need.

The statutory guidance identifies seven key aspects to the DASS role (DH, 2006a, s7.1):

- accountability for assessing local needs and ensuring availability and delivery of a full range of local authority services;
- professional leadership, including workforce planning;
- leading the implementation of standards;
- managing cultural change;
- promoting local access and ownership and driving partnership working;
- delivering an integrated whole systems approach to supporting communities;
- promoting social inclusion and wellbeing.

The DASS is expected to:

> ... work closely with the full range of providers of community services and benefits, including Supporting People/housing support, leisure services, adult education, community safety and the independent, voluntary and community sector as well as with Primary Care Trusts (PCTs) and other NHS [National Health Service] organisations to take a whole systems approach to providing care and supporting wellbeing. (DH, 2006b, para 11)

They are also expected to work through Local Strategic Partnerships and Local Area Agreements to influence partners beyond the traditional boundaries of local government departments. A particular boundary exists with health:

> The aim is to move to a position where there is clear accountability and a strategy that is integrated across health and social care, for adult social care, both locally and nationally and a holistic focus on the needs of adults. The DASS should be responsible for ensuring the quality of adult social care services across the local authority area in all sectors, irrespective of whether or not services are provided directly by the local authority. This includes ensuring that professional and occupational standards are maintained. (DH, 2006b, para 13)

Suggestions are also given for a much broader well-being focus to the DASS role, embracing for example further, higher and adult education, leisure, housing, and community services:

> Increasingly, multi-agency approaches will be needed to support the wellbeing of communities and expanding the remit of the officer responsible for the DASS function may provide for a more holistic approach to meeting the needs of people in the local community. (DH, 2006b, para 47)

The range of individuals included within the remit of the DASS is wide: people with physical frailty due to ageing; people with physical disabilities; people with sensory impairment; people with learning disabilities; people with mental health needs (including mental frailty due to old age); people with long-term medical conditions requiring social care in addition to healthcare; people with autism spectrum disorder; Deafblind people; older people with mental health problems, or learning disabilities; people who misuse substances; people who have experienced domestic violence; people living with HIV; offenders; people with no fixed abode; homeless households; and asylum seekers.

In establishing these two posts and their associated directorates, the two sets of guidance sought both to highlight additional areas that might be embraced within the respective remits and to identify potential areas of overlap and collaboration. 'The relationship between these two posts will be crucial to ensuring that the needs of both adults and children in families are met and that services work well together' (DH, 2007, para 2.7). Key areas of transition are given particular prominence:

> The DCS should work closely with the DASS to support
> young people with social care needs during the transition
> to the adult social services system; identify any adults in
> contact with social services who are parents or carers and
> ensure the needs of their children are taken into account;
> and ensure a co-ordinated approach to meeting the care
> needs of communities. (draft guidance, DCSF, 2008, para
> 3.9)

The two Directors are also asked to ensure that clear protocols are
agreed to support joint working and a collaborative approach to
meeting the lifelong needs of all people supported by social services.

An interesting development has been an emerging trend in England
towards the appointment of Directors with combined responsibilities
for both children's and adults' services. Linked to this is often the
reintegration of a number of core support services. At the time of
writing it is thought that this strategy has been adopted by up to
10% of English local authorities including Bracknell Forest, Ealing,
East Riding of Yorkshire, Havering, Medway, Redcar and Cleveland,
Stockton-on-Tees, Wakefield and West Sussex.

The Improvement and Development Agency (IDeA, 2008)
interviewed 10 joint Directors with a view to assessing the advantages
and disadvantages of a combined model. From the detailed accounts
of individual activity, a number of more general points emerge. The
key driver where the model has been adopted has been to focus more
effectively on the family and to provide more integrated and cross-
cutting services. *Think family, think community* was the title of the IDeA
report and encapsulates the ambition of a holistic perspective for
vulnerable families. The possibility of achieving some cost efficiencies
in a combined directorate was also a consideration in some areas,
together with a desire to avoid some of the gaps emerging through
the separation of services. Cross-fertilisation was also valued – one
joint Director commented: 'there's a lot that children's services can
learn from the adult's world in terms of fully delivering on integration
... and the emerging safeguarding agenda in adults' services can learn
a huge amount from children's services' (IDeA, 2008, p 5). Another
commented: 'we're beginning to see results around inter-generational
work, in terms of being able to focus on localities and on families where
there are several areas of the directorate involved' (2008, p 28).

Other areas highlighted by those operating in this way included
more streamlined partnership working with external agencies and
the benefits of a joint strategic needs assessment that addressed both

children and adults. Of particular relevance was the opportunity for a smoother care pathway for children with complex needs. This could include the opportunity to step outside traditional age-related transition points. For example, in West Sussex the possibility of alternative age groupings such as 0-14 and 15-25 was being considered: 'for a child with disability, 18 is probably not a very good cut-off point for transfer from children's to adults' services' (2008, p 6). It may be of note that many of the councils who had combined responsibilities were rated among the best in the country for adults' and children's services.

It is important to recognise that the combined posts are not a return to the former Directors of Social Services. John Dixon, Executive Director of Adults and Children at West Sussex Council has explained: 'It's not back to the old model. The big difference is that education and social services have come together, and are responsible for schools. It is a two step process and we are now seeing the second step' (*Community Care*, 22 July 2008). Another Director has commented: 'It is not contradictory to *Every Child Matters*. Rather, it means the council can concentrate on tailoring services for families, and for people from birth to end of life' (*Community Care*, 22 July 2008). The opportunity to pursue the Think Family agenda is perhaps one of the strongest arguments: 'almost all children with complex problems have adults attached to them who also have complex needs. So there is a strong case for an integrated adult and children's response' (*Community Care*, 22 July 2008). Adult services Directors have often assumed responsibility for areas such as housing and neighbourhood renewal and/or leisure that are of equal importance for children.

Despite these developments, the draft statutory guidance on the role of the DCS does not appear to be supportive. Para 3.10 (DCSF, 2008) states:

> There are clear distinctions between the roles and statutory responsibilities of the DCS and the DASS. While it is legally permissible for a local authority to combine the role of DCS with the role of the DASS, it is not recommended without a very strong justification. Any local authority taking this decision should ensure that its structures fully integrate education and children's social care. It should not have a second tier structure spilt distinctly into education and social services.

Moreover, authorities are exhorted 'to consider very carefully whether such an extension of the role would still permit the DCS to provide sufficient personal focus to the well-being of children in the local area' (DCSF, 2008, para 3.11).

Health

The NHS has experienced a variety of configurations over its lifetime. The current structure in England embraces strategic health authorities and a range of different types of trusts. Strategic health authorities were created in 2002 to manage the NHS locally and provide a key link with the Department of Health. An initial 28 authorities were reduced in 2006 to 10. Strategic health authorities are responsible for:

- developing plans for improving health services in their local area;
- making sure that local health services are of a high quality and are performing well;
- increasing the capacity of local health services so that they can provide more services;
- making sure that national priorities – for example programmes for improving cancer services – are integrated into local health service plans.

In terms of trusts, a key distinction is between the acute trusts (176 in number at the time of writing) managing acute hospitals, and the primary care trusts (152 in number) providing the majority of community services and controlling 80% of the NHS budget. In addition, there are 60 specific mental health trusts, providing health and social care trusts for people with mental health problems. A particularly interesting initiative has been the development of care trusts, uniting health and social care for adults (Glasby and Peck, 2004). Their growth, however, has been much slower than originally anticipated, 10 at the time of writing, with five of these also fitting the category of mental health trusts (Camden and Islington Mental Health and Social Care Trust, Bradford District, Manchester, Sandwell and Sheffield). Most recently, there has been the development of foundation trusts, a new type of NHS hospital run by local managers, staff and members of the public, which is tailored to the needs of the local population. NHS foundation trust status is open to acute, specialist, mental health and care trusts. First introduced in 2004, 115 trusts had been granted foundation status at the time of writing.

Scotland

In Scotland, the duty placed on local authorities under the 1968 Social Work (Scotland) Act to 'promote social welfare' continues to be delivered through social work departments embracing both children and adults. Their focus is on:

- services to children, young people and families;
- community services that allow individuals to remain in their own homes;
- criminal justice services including supervision and rehabilitation of offenders.

The last of these is distinct from England where there is a separate probation service; the services are, however, funded by a central grant direct from the Scottish Government. Eight community justice authorities have also been created with the aim of providing a coordinated approach to the planning and monitoring of offender services. The membership includes police forces, NHS boards, the Scottish Prison Service and Victim Support Scotland.

Some local authorities have separate social work departments; others have merged social work with other departments such as education or housing. Integration has been a prominent theme. *For Scotland's children*, produced by the Scottish Executive in 2001 (Scottish Executive, 2001), proposed a single service system with joint workforce planning, joint service planning and a multidisciplinary preventative approach to assessment and intervention. *Getting it right for every child: Proposals for action 2005* (Scottish Executive, 2005) set out an integrated assessment planning and recording framework for all children.

Collaboration with health around adult support has been more centrally directed in Scotland than in England, most particularly through the Joint Future Agenda (Petch, 2008). A fundamental review of social work provision was completed in 2006, *Changing lives: The report of the 21st century social work review* (Scottish Executive, 2006). This concluded:

> The ability of local authorities and their planning partners to integrate services around the needs of people who use services is constrained by overly complex governance and funding arrangements. In practice, this often means that success is only achieved through compromise and considerable effort and goodwill to negotiate complex

systems. If integrated working is to become the norm, then greater clarity and direction on governance and funding arrangements is required at national level. (Scottish Executive, 2006, p 46)

Health provision in Scotland is the responsibility of the 14 health boards and the associated acute and primary care trusts. Most recently, community health partnerships have been established, 40 in total, seeking to maximise the opportunities for integrated working across health and social care.

Wales

The organisation of social services in Wales follows that of Scotland in retaining departments that deliver support to both adults and children. Each of the 22 local authorities has a Director of Social Services. Below them there are 22 adult service heads and 22 heads for children's services. The Social Services Improvement Agency provides an overarching role. A 10-year social services strategy, *Fulfilled lives, supportive communities*, was published by the Welsh Assembly Government in 2007 (WAG, 2007a), and there is *The strategy for older people in Wales* (WAG, 2003), *Raising the standard* (WAG, 2005) – for adults with mental health problems – and a Learning Disability Strategy (WAG, 2007b). Six National Service Frameworks are in place: for children, coronary heart disease, diabetes, renal health, mental health and older people.

Health services in Wales are being reorganised from October 2009. Six local health boards plus the existing Powys trust are replacing the former 22 primary-focused local health boards and the seven NHS trusts that ran acute and community services and mental health services for older people. The focus of the reorganisation is on integration, abolishing the boundaries between the boards and trusts, between in- and out-of-hospital care, and between primary, community and acute provision. The internal market has been scrapped, with services being planned by NHS Wales in collaboration with the boards.

Northern Ireland

Northern Ireland has traditionally been heralded for its integrated structure for health and social services – although it is probably fair to say that more systematic examination of its impact has been rare. Unlike the rest of the UK, local authorities are not responsible for personal social services. The 1972 Health and Personal Social Services

(NI) Order paved the way for four health and social services boards, taking over welfare functions from defunct county and county borough councils and the Northern Ireland Hospitals Authority with 26 local Hospital Management Committees, which were also abolished. In 1989, the UK government White Paper *Working for patients* (DH, 1989) led to the 1991 Health and Personal Social Services (Northern Ireland) Order. This order created new health and social services trusts, which were given responsibility for delivering services. The existing boards adapted to a commissioning role through contracts with the new trusts. New health and social services councils were also created to monitor actions of boards and take up complaints.

Most recently, a new health and social services authority, the Department of Health, Social Services and Public Safety, has been created to cover the whole of Northern Ireland and to take on the functions of boards from April 2008. It commissions services using seven new local commissioning groups and five 'super' health and social care trusts, which replaced the 18 existing trusts from April 2007. These cover Belfast, Northern, Southern, South East and Western and combine acute and community health with social services. The commissioning groups match a reduced number of district councils, down from 26 to seven.

Throughout the UK, a number of specific arrangements are in place for particular groups, often those who, as will be seen in subsequent chapters, are particularly the focus for transition arrangements. The *Valuing people* White Paper (DH, 2001), for example, required Learning Disability Partnership Boards to be set up in every local authority in England by October 2001. In Scotland, *The same as you?* (Scottish Executive, 2000) heralded the establishment of Partnership in Practice Agreements (PIPs). Plans for the delivery of learning disability and mental health services in Wales are currently under review, with consultation at the end of 2008 on proposals for a single national board, supported by regional boards, to plan and provide all mental health, learning disability and substance misuse services in Wales.

Other agencies

Alongside health and social care, housing provides the third essential element of support. Structures for social housing vary considerably across the four constituent countries of the UK. In Northern Ireland, there is a single central body with responsibility for public housing – the Northern Ireland Housing Executive. In Wales, each of the 22 local authorities has housing within its remit, while in England, housing is the responsibility of district and metropolitan borough councils, of unitary authorities and of the 33 London boroughs – a total of 354 agencies. Housing in Scotland became the responsibility of the 32 unitary local authorities created in 1996; since 2003, a number of authorities (currently six) have passed their responsibilities to registered social landlords, for example the Glasgow Housing Agency.

For those moving between children's and adults' services, a key agency is Connexions, established to provide information and advice to young people between the ages of 18 and 24. The New Deal, part of the Department for Work and Pensions, is designed for those who have been claiming Jobseeker's Allowance for six or more months. The New Deal for Disabled People provides a network of job brokers chosen by JobCentre Plus who offer particular experience in supporting young disabled people to find work.

Notwithstanding the variation in organisational arrangements throughout the UK, a common theme for those caught up in a process of transition is for the agencies to which they are looking for support and guidance to work in partnership. The potential for partnership working grows ever more wide, embracing collaboration both across statutory agencies and with a wide variety of independent sector agencies, including both voluntary and private providers. There is a wide literature on the pitfalls and potential of such collaboration, too extensive to be detailed here. The key imperative, however, for those caught in transition is that the organisational structures should facilitate rather than constrain the support that is required. Local Strategic Partnerships and Local Area Agreements, recent initiatives in England, exemplify the increased focus on areas both defining local priorities and working in partnership to respond to these priorities.

Case study examples

At the conference that was an early trigger for this volume, a number of case studies were presented of ways in which local authorities were seeking to bridge potential gaps, both between children's and adults' departments and with other agencies. These case studies are presented as a preliminary to the exploration of policy and practice in specific areas of transition explored in subsequent chapters.

Telford

Telford presented a snapshot of the interaction between the children's and adults' services, detailing strategies at each of three levels: governance, management and operational. In terms of *governance*, there was representation from adult services on the Children and Young Persons Strategic Plan, and from children's services on the health and well-being partnership. Also established were a joint commissioning unit, an autism working group, action learning sets, and work around Supporting People. For *management*, there were quarterly meetings and additional meetings for key managers; transition protocols; and clusters of activity around parenting programmes and the Building Schools for the Future programme. The transition protocols included both an overarching protocol with an appeals mechanism, and detailed specific proposals relating, first, to learning disabilities and children with complex needs and, second, to child and adolescent mental health services. At *operational* level, activity focused on four key areas: adult and child protection with a safeguards advisory service; the emergency duty team; children's occupational therapy; and transition workers.

Southampton

Southampton reflected on an experience where an earlier transition policy had been developed but failed to be fully implemented. They identified a number of factors that inhibit effective transition:

- the need for detailed protocols and senior management involvement;
- resources for young people with multiple lower-level difficulties;
- professional mistrust;
- conflicting professional philosophies across adult and children's services;
- increasing numbers at the same time as static or reducing resources;
- complexities of health;
- the need to plan ahead;
- financial factors.

The last of these is of course a key factor. Continuing care criteria can create a major disjuncture between adult and children's services, while young people defined as vulnerable by children's services may not meet the critical or substantial categories of the Fair Access to Care Services criteria operated by many adult services. For young care leavers there is the question of who is the corporate parent.

Plymouth

Plymouth outlined their configuration of services for people with sensory impairment and its attempt to embrace both adults' and children's services. The sensory team comprised a social worker for sensory impaired people, two staff providing equipment for hearing impaired individuals, three staff registering and providing rehabilitation services to visually impaired people and a community care worker working with Deafblind service users. In the past the previous social worker for Deaf people had worked with both the sensory team and the children with disability team for 18 months. The different eligibility criteria of the two teams had presented challenges, with the children's team not working with children with solely a sensory impairment. The sensory team had therefore developed a relationship with the education sensory team who worked in schools with children with a visual or hearing impairment. The sensory team made a particular contribution in terms of registration for visually impaired children and support to parents. Twice yearly the education team attended one of the team meetings to sustain the network.

A parallel development was the development of a protocol between children's services, the Learning Disability Partnership, the education department and Connexions. This was a multiagency document specifying responsibilities and timescales for each party. From this developed a broad-based transition group, with a transitions worker appointed in 2007. The group itself consists of the care leavers manager, the children with disabilities team managers from occupational therapy and social care, the learning disability team managers from social care and the primary care trust, the special schools worker, the person-centred planning trainer, the Children and Adolescent Mental Health Services (CAMHS) coordinator, the adult social care team leaders for occupational therapy, social care and the sensory team, the Plymouth City Connexions team manager and the ward manager from the children's hospital. The transition protocol was rewritten and person-centred plans were developed linked to the statementing process. An information booklet was produced for parents and children, addressing key issues of rights, eligibility criteria and capacity issues as children become adults.

Against this backcloth, a sensory transition service was developed. Every quarter the group meets to allocate assessments by adult services, with the opportunity to discuss the most appropriate allocation of complex cases. Following the assessment there is feedback to the group on the possible services required and an initial individual profile for the transition of the young adult is produced by the social worker from the children's disability team. The sensory practitioner link worker for hearing impaired services networks with other practitioners to be aware of the other services that are currently working with the young person and attends transition reviews as required. The occupational therapy and social care team leaders from the transition group have produced a spreadsheet that shows the young person's age and present services involved. The aim is to prioritise cases by age, allocate cases to adult social care assessment teams based on the young person's address, develop a protocol and recording system for young people in transition that will receive future services from adult services, and aggregate needs to inform future resource requirements. At present, young people are being assessed at the age of 17; in future the plan is to assess young people at the age of 14.

Three case studies illustrate the complexities that such collaborations need to address:

• Case study one

Connexions informed the local authority that a 19-year-old attending a special school no longer had a Statement. However, the Learning Skills Council had agreed to pay for an extra two years' education. The local authority was being asked to pay for transport to enable the young person to attend the school in two weeks' time. The sensory team did not hold a community care budget and needed to sell the case to the assessment team budget holders.

• Case study two

A young Deafblind person was in further education after returning from a school for Deaf people but was socially isolated at home, with a family that felt stressed most of the time. At college there was a complete misunderstanding of her complex needs, due to a lack of coordination and information not being shared with all the relevant organisations. The sensory team staff assessed the situation with a Carer's Assessment and an assessment of the young person. Ultimately, a Direct Payment provided a Guide Communicator to enable the young person to spend more time outside the family environment and to give her parents time together. The further education college was given the relevant information to understand and meet the young person's special needs.

• Case study three

A young man with learning disabilities and registered as blind was approaching 18. He attended a school for young people with little or no sight as a weekly boarder. He was being supported by the children with disability team, with respite care for his mother during the school holidays and mobility training from the education sensory team also during the school holidays. The transition group allocated the adult social care assessment jointly to the learning disability and sensory services and information was gathered for the 'Individual Profile for Transition of Young Adult' form provided by the children with disability team and current records held by the learning disability team and the education sensory team. The school had completed a transition review in March 2006. The individual had an education statement from December 1995, which had subsequently been reviewed.

A joint assessment visit to the school was made in February 2007 by the sensory team member and the learning disability assessment team leader. Both visited the mother in March 2007 to complete the assessment. The assessment showed that the young man needed constant one-to-one assistance with personal care. He cannot see his food and tends to sniff it prior to putting it into his mouth. He has little verbal communication and expresses himself when in pain by grabbing others. He is able to orientate himself within familiar indoor surroundings. He needs one-to-one assistance when outdoors to mobilise on stairs/steps, getting in and out of cars and general orientation. He enjoys the company of the staff group and is tolerant of his fellow pupils.

The outcome of the assessment was that the individual will need a lifetime placement in residential or supported housing, paid for by the learning disability service. SENSE or Seeability would be engaged by the education sensory team to assess the young man's future accommodation needs. He would need adult social care assistance once he reached the age of 19. He would stay at school until 21 if the Learning Skills Council paid for his tuition after the Statement ceased at 19. Adult social care would need to pay for the transport at weekends and school holidays with the respite care and mobility training.

A number of general points can be drawn from these case examples:

* the importance of senior staff support;
* the importance of the involvement of young people and their families;
* the benefits of a local programme providing the right services for local people;
* the importance of agreement on the ways to work together;
* the importance of a focus on the person and their needs;
* the importance of regular reviews of the transition plan.

References

DCSF (Department for Children, Schools and Families) (2005) *Statutory guidance on the role and responsibilities of the Director of Children's Services and Lead Member for Children's Services*, London: DCSF.

DCSF (2008) *Statutory guidance: The roles and responsibilities of the Lead Member for Children's Services and the Director of Children's Services – Consultation*, London: DCSF.

DfES (Department for Education and Skills) (2003) *Every Child Matters*, Cm 5860, London: The Stationery Office.

DH (Department of Health) (1989) *Working for patients*, Cm 555, London: HMSO.

DH (2001) *Valuing people: A new strategy for learning disability for the 21st century*, Cm 5086, London: The Stationery Office.

DH (2006a) *Guidance on the statutory Chief Officer post of the Director of Adult Social Services*, London: DH.

DH (2006b) *Best practice guidance on the role of the Director of Adult Social Services*, London: DH.

DH (2006c) *Our health, our care, our say*, London: The Stationery Office.

DH (2007) *Independence, well-being and choice: Our vision for the future of social care*, London: The Stationery Office.

Glasby, J. and Peck, E. (2004) *Care trusts: Partnership working in action*, Oxford: Radcliffe Publishing.

IDeA (Improvement and Development Agency) (2008) *Think family, think community: The role of Directors with combined responsibilities for children's and adults' services*, London: IDeA.

Lord Laming (2003) *The Victoria Climbié Inquiry*, Cm 5730, London: The Stationery Office.

Petch, A. (2008) *Health and social care: Establishing a joint future?*, Edinburgh: Dunedin Academic Press.

Scottish Executive (2000) *The same as you? A review of services for people with learning disabilities*, Edinburgh: Scottish Executive.

Scottish Executive (2001) *For Scotland's children: Better integrated children's services*, Edinburgh: Scottish Executive.

Scottish Executive (2005) *Getting it right for every child: Proposals for action*, Edinburgh: Scottish Executive.

Scottish Executive (2006) *Changing lives: The report of the 21st century social work review*, Edinburgh: Scottish Executive

WAG (Welsh Assembly Government) (2003) *The strategy for older people in Wales*, Cardiff: WAG.

WAG (2005) *Raising the standard*, Cardiff: WAG.

WAG (2007a) *Fulfilled lives, supportive communities: A strategy for social services*, Cardiff: WAG.

WAG (2007b) *Statement on the policy and practice for adults with a learning disability*, Cardiff: WAG.

THREE

Young people leaving care: transitions to adulthood

Mike Stein

Introduction

For most young people today, their journey from being a young person to becoming an adult means they have to travel on a number of pathways: from leaving school to entering further or higher education, employment or training; from dependency on their birth families to living on their own, or with others, and for some young people, becoming a young parent; from living in the family home to becoming a householder in their own right; and, both underpinned and potentially reinforced by these transitions, developing their own identity and a positive sense of well-being.

It is a journey from restricted to full citizenship, derived in part by lifecourse choices, from which adult rights and responsibilities flow, but it is also mediated by structural constraints such as socioeconomic background, ethnicity, sex and disability. The purpose of this chapter is to explore how young people who have been looked after make the transition to adulthood.

Who are young people leaving care?

Official UK data reveal that 10,118 young people aged 16 and over left care in England, Northern Ireland, Scotland and Wales, in the year ending March 2007, just under 2,000 more than in the year ending March 2003. In 2007, more young people in Scotland left care aged 16 and 17 than aged 18 and over, whereas in England and Northern Ireland, more young people left care at 18 years of age than at 16 or 17. In England, more young people left care from foster care than residential care, whereas in Scotland, more young people left care from a residential placement than foster care. However, regional data from within the four UK countries show considerable variation in the number of care leavers, their final placements and the length of time they have spent in care before leaving (DHSSPS (NI), 2007; NAW, 2007; Scottish Government, 2007; DCSF, 2008a).

Care leavers' transitions

Education, employment and training

Analysis of the Youth Cohort Study carried out for England and Wales shows that there is a clear association between post-16 educational achievement and the pathway to well-paid more secure employment (DfES, 2001). Conversely, young people who leave school at the minimum leaving age (currently 16) are at greater risk of poverty and subsequent social exclusion. Both research and official performance data for care leavers in the UK have consistently revealed lower levels of educational attainment at age 16 and 18, lower post-16 participation rates, and higher levels of unemployment, than for young people in the general population (Gibbs et al, 2005). However, in England, there is evidence of some progress in GCSE (General Certificate of Secondary Education) performance – although not at the same rate as for other young people – and in the proportions of young people participating in post-16 education and employment, since the introduction of the Children (Leaving Care) Act in October 2001 (Broad, 2005; DCSF, 2008a). But a significant gap remains (DCSF, 2008b). The relatively high proportion of care leavers not engaged in education, employment or training, as well as the low-paid employment of many others, results in many young people struggling on relatively low incomes.

Leaving care and setting up home

Birth families, including members of the extended family network, provide a lot of assistance to young people when setting up their own home. Financial, practical and emotional support, as well as returning home at times of difficulty, not only greatly assists young people but also protects them from poverty and homelessness (Jones, 2002). However, many young people leaving care are faced with the challenge of managing their accommodation at just 16-18 years of age. They are more likely than those of a similar age to move regularly and be overrepresented among the young homeless population. A 2001 Scottish survey showed that 61% of care leavers had moved three or more times, and 40% had reported having been homeless since leaving care (Dixon and Stein, 2005). Research comparing homeless with non-homeless young people found that those who were homeless were 10 times more likely to have been in care during childhood and that between a quarter and a third of rough sleepers were once in care (Craig, 1996; SEU, 1998). However, being settled in accommodation is associated with a positive sense of well-being, and can to some extent compensate care leavers for earlier disruption in their lives (Dixon, 2008).

Leaving care, social networks and parenthood

Research carried out in England shows that most young people leaving care had very poor relationships with their families, which ruled out a return home — although not necessarily contact: less than a third of young people had positive supportive relationships with one or both parents during their transition from care, but within 18-24 months of leaving there was a *rapprochement* and this had increased to a half. However, the same study found that that the majority of young people were socially isolated and almost entirely dependent on the support of professionals (Biehal and Wade, 1996).

Teenage motherhood is associated with a high risk of poverty through reduced employment opportunities, dependency on benefits, social housing, as well as poorer physical and mental health (Hobcraft and Kiernan, 1999). Research carried out in England, Scotland and Northern Ireland showed that young women care leavers, aged 16-19, were more likely to be young parents than other women of their age group (Gibbs et al, 2005). Both having young children (if the youngest child is under five) and being a young mother (under 25) is also associated with poverty (DWP, 2004). A study of intergenerational transmission of social exclusion estimates that young people who have been in care are two and a half times more likely to become adolescent parents than other young people, and data from the British Cohort Study indicates that children of women who have spent time in care themselves are two and a half times more likely to go into care than their peers (Hobcraft, 1998; Cheesebrough, 2002).

Young parenthood, under certain conditions, may also be beneficial. The gains for some have included reduced isolation, a renewal of family links and improved relationships with their mothers and their partners' families. However, a qualitative study of young mothers who had been in care found that they faced a range of problems including financial difficulties, accessing services and coping with parenthood as well as leaving care (Biehal and Wade, 1996; Chase et al, 2003).

Leaving care, mental health and well-being

Children and young people who become looked after are subject to many of the risk factors associated with the development of mental health problems: lone and young parenthood; reconstituted families; severe marital distress; low income; overcrowding or large family size; paternal criminality; and maternal psychiatric disorder (Koprowska and Stein, 2000). The Office for National Statistics (ONS) surveys for the mental health of young people aged 5-17 living in private households and being looked after, in England showed that looked-after young people, aged 11-15, were four to five times more likely to have a mental disorder than those living in private households: 49% compared with 11% (Melzer et al, 2003). Analysis of the UK data from the National Child Development Study indicated a higher risk of depression at age 23 and 33, a higher incidence of psychiatric and personality disorder and greater levels of emotional and behavioural problems among those who had been in care, than for those of the same-age population who had not (Cheung and Buchanan, 1997). There is also evidence that care leavers are more likely than other young people to have drug and alcohol problems, be involved in offending behaviour and be overrepresented in custody (Newburn et al, 2002; CSCI, 2007; DCSF, 2007).

Research has also shown that transitions from care can combine with earlier pre-care and in-care difficulties in affecting overall health and well-being. The same study also highlighted the links between mental health and general well-being, as well as other dimensions of young people's lives such as risk behaviour and progress in finding a home and embarking on a career – highlighting the interconnectedness of young people's lives (Dixon, 2008).

Transitions and social exclusion

For many care leavers, the transitions to adulthood, or citizenship, discussed above, are often pathways to social exclusion in terms of both material disadvantage and marginalisation. Specific groups of care leavers may face additional disadvantages due to their status or characteristics, compounding their exclusion. Black and minority ethnic young people, including those of mixed heritage, face similar challenges to other young people leaving care. However, they may also experience identity problems derived from a lack of knowledge of their heritage, or loss of contact with family and community, as well as the impact of racism and discrimination (Barn et al, 2005).

Research carried out during 2002–03 in England found that unaccompanied refugee and asylum-seeking young people were excluded from services under the 2000 Children (Leaving Care) Act where local authorities decided not to 'look after' them but support them under Section 17 of the 1989 Children Act. They were also likely to receive poorer services than looked-after young people, especially in respect of support from leaving care teams (Wade et al, 2005).

Young disabled people may experience inadequate planning and poor consultation, and their transitions from care may be abrupt or delayed by restricted housing and employment options and poor support aftercare (Rabiee et al, 2001; Priestley et al, 2003).

The research evidence on transitions, organised within a social exclusion framework, has contributed to a greater awareness of the reduced life chances of care leavers, and their links with other excluded groups, as well as providing a focus for policy intervention. However, these transitions need to be contextualised as part of the lifecourse of young people leaving care. It is as a consequence of their pre-care, in-care and leaving-care experiences that many care leavers are predisposed to poor life chances. Also, the application of a lifecourse perspective can assist in identifying from research what contributes to positive outcomes, and can support the transitions of care leavers.

Transitions and the lifecourse of care leavers

Pre-care experiences

The disadvantaged social class position of families from which many young people enter care and the associated cultural barriers will have a major influence on their educational achievement, especially for those young people who enter care during their school years (Berridge, 2007). In addition, most of these young people will have experienced damaging intra-family relations that may have included neglect and poor parenting, or physical, emotional or sexual abuse, experiences that are likely to impact on their later emotional and intellectual development.

Care experiences

Against this background, the purpose of care should be to compensate these young people. The foundation stone is stability. However, a consistent finding from research studies of young people leaving care, carried out between 1980 and 2004, has been their experience of instability and placement disruption following their initial or later separation from their birth families: in these studies, 30–40% of young people had four plus moves and within this group 6–10% had a very large number of moves, as many as 10 or more (Stein, 2005)

As detailed above, both official data and research studies show low levels of attainment and participation beyond the minimum school-leaving age. There is research evidence that good outcomes are associated with placement stability, being looked after longer, more often achieved in foster care placements, a carer committed to helping the young person, including their own family; and a supportive and encouraging environment for study (Biehal et al, 1995). There is also evidence that young people who have had several placements can achieve educational success if they remain in the same school – and this also means that they are able to maintain friendships and contacts with helpful teachers (Jackson and Thomas, 2001).

Stability and encouragement are also associated with success in post-16 employment, education and training. Young people who left care earlier, at 16 and 17, had more unsettled careers and were more likely to be unemployed, and those young people with mental health problems and emotional and behavioural difficulties were particularly vulnerable to poor outcomes (Wade and Dixon, 2006). Young people who went on to higher education were more likely to have had a stable care experience, continuity in their schooling and encouragement by their birth parents, even though they were unable to care for them, and were greatly assisted by their foster carers in their schooling (Ajayi and Quigley, 2006).

The process of transition

The first part of this chapter discussed the main transitions made by young people leaving care during their journey to adulthood, in particular detailing the differences between care leavers and other young people. But how do young people leaving care experience the process of transition?

As detailed above, a consistent finding from studies of care leavers is that a majority move to independent living at between 16 and 18 years of age, whereas most of their peers remain at home well into their twenties (Stein, 2004). They are expected to undertake their journey to adulthood, from restricted to full citizenship, far younger and in far less time than their peers. For many of these young people, leaving care is a final event and there is no option to return in times of difficulty. Also, they often have to cope with major status changes in their lives at the time of leaving care, as detailed above: leaving foster care or their children's home and setting up a new home, often in a new area, and for some young people starting a family as well; leaving school and finding their way into further education, training or employment, or coping with unemployment. They are denied the psychological opportunity and space to focus, or to deal with issues over time, which is how most young people cope with the challenges of transition (Coleman and Hendry, 1999). In short, their journey to adulthood is both accelerated and compressed.

As the UK's Joseph Rowntree Foundation's Young People in Transition research programme shows, during the last 20 years, patterns of transition into adulthood have been changing fast: a major decline in the youth labour market based on manufacturing and apprenticeship training; an extension of youth training, further and higher education; and a reduction in entitlements to universal welfare benefits for young people (Jones, 2002). These changes have resulted in young people being more dependent on their families for emotional, financial and practical support, often into their early twenties. In today's 'risk' society, parents, grandparents and other relatives are increasingly occupying a central role at different life stages, yet, young people leaving care, who are the most likely to lack the range and depth of help given by families, are expected to cope at a far younger age than young people living with their families.

Ethnographic research also highlights the significance of transition for young people during their journey to adulthood (Hart, 1984; Horrocks, 2002). The process of social transition has traditionally included three distinct, but related stages: leaving or disengagement; transition itself; and integration into a new or different social state. In post (or late?) modern societies, providing more opportunities but also more risks, this process has become more extended and less structured, although the 'activities' associated with the three stages still remain. But for many young people leaving care, there is the expectation of instant adulthood. They often miss out on the critical preparation stage to the transition itself, which gives young people an opportunity to 'space out', and provides a time for freedom, exploration, reflection, risk taking and identity search. For a majority of young people today this is gained through the experience of further and, especially, higher education but many care leavers, as a consequence of their pre-care and care experience are unable to take advantage of these educational opportunities. Also, as discussed above, in the context of extended transitions, the family plays an increasing role in providing financial, practical and emotional support. But for many care leavers their family relationships at this time may be missing or problematic rather than supportive.

Transitions in the context of the lifecourse of care leavers

A review of research studies of young people leaving care during the last 20 years, including international research, identifies three broad groups of care leavers: those whose transitions to adulthood, have, in the main been successful; those whose transitions have been more mixed; and those whose transitions have led to very poor outcomes (Stein, 2006; Stein and Munro, 2008).

The first group – those young people 'moving on' successfully from care – were likely to have had stability and continuity in their lives; made sense of their family relationships so they could psychologically move on from them; and achieved some educational success before leaving care. Their preparation had been gradual, they had left care later and their moving on was likely to have been planned. Participating in further or higher education, having a job they liked or being a parent themselves, played a significant part in 'feeling normal'. The 'moving on' group welcomed the challenge of independent living and gaining more control over their lives. They saw this as improving their confidence and self-esteem. In general, their resilience had been enhanced by their experiences while living in, leaving and after care. They had been able to make good use of the help they had been offered, often maintaining contact and support from former carers. In most respects, their transitions to adulthood reflected normative patterns.

The second group – the 'survivors' – had more mixed transitions from care. They had experienced more instability, movement and disruption while living in care than the 'moving on' group. They were also likely to leave care younger, with few or no qualifications, and often following a breakdown in foster care or a sudden exit from their children's home. They were likely to experience further movement and problems after leaving care, including periods of homelessness, low-paid casual or short-term, unfulfilling work and unemployment. They were also likely to experience problems in their personal and professional relationships through patterns of detachment and dependency. Many in this group saw themselves as 'more tough', as having done things 'off my own back' and as 'survivors' since leaving care. They believed that the many problems they had faced, and often were still coping with, had made them more grown-up and self-reliant – although their view of themselves as independent was often contradicted by the reality of high degrees of agency dependency for assistance with accommodation, money and personal problems.

There is research evidence that what assisted their transitions was the personal and professional support they received after leaving care (Dixon and Stein, 2005). Specialist leaving care workers and key workers could assist these young people. Also, mentoring, including mentoring by ex-care young people (or peer mentoring) may assist young people during their journey to independence, and offer them a different type of relationship from professional support or troubled family relationships (Clayden and Stein, 2005). Helping young people in finding and maintaining their accommodation can be critical to their mental health and well-being during transition. Families may also help, but returning to them may prove very problematic for some young people (Sinclair et al, 2005). Overall, some combination of personal and professional support networks could help them overcome their very poor starting points at the time of leaving care and aid their transition.

The third group of care leavers was the most disadvantaged and had the most difficult transitions from care to adulthood. They had the most damaging pre-care family experiences and, in the main, care was unable to compensate them, or to help them overcome their past difficulties. Their lives in care were likely to include many further placement moves and the associated disruption to their lives, especially in relation to their personal relationships and education. They were also likely to have a cluster of difficulties while in care that often began earlier, including emotional and behavioural difficulties, problems at school and getting into trouble (Wade and Dixon, 2006). They were the least likely to have a redeeming relationship with a family member or carer, and were likely to leave care younger, following a placement breakdown. At the time of leaving care, their life chances were very poor indeed. After leaving care, they were likely to be unemployed, become homeless and have great difficulties in maintaining their accommodation. They were also highly likely to be lonely, isolated and have mental health problems, often being defined by projects as 'young people with very complex needs'. Aftercare support was unlikely to be able to help them overcome their very poor starting points and they also lacked or alienated personal support. But it was important to these young people that somebody was there for them.

Transitions and improving outcomes: key policy and practice points

Assisting young people at home

The starting point is to prevent young people from going into care. Research shows that preventative services for children and young people *'on the edge of care'* are currently limited (Biehal, 2005). They should be part of a continuum of services that include 'early' interventions in the development of problems, as well as more intensive responses to crisis and follow-up support. Problems of early onset may persist during transition into adulthood and there are also a range of problems that commonly emerge for the first time during adolescence (for example, mental health problems or substance misuse). The provision of a service at an earlier stage, before problems reach crisis point, may prevent the escalation of difficulties for many children and young people.

Improving the quality of care

This will mean providing better-quality care to compensate young people for their damaging pre-care experiences through:

- stability and continuity;
- a positive sense of identity and well-being;
- assistance to overcome educational deficits, including maximising young people's opportunities to make progress, paying equal attention to the care and educational needs of young people;
- the provision of holistic preparation, addressing the practical, personal and social needs of young people.

As discussed above, there is evidence that good-quality foster carers and small children's homes with a positive culture can assist young people to achieve positive outcomes.

Transitions from care

Young people leaving care should be provided with opportunities for more gradual transitions from care – less accelerated and compressed – more akin to normative transitions. This will include giving young people 'psychological space' and recognising the three different stages of transition – leaving, transition itself and integration – common to the normative experience of emerging adulthood, in contrast to the 'instant

---

adulthood', experienced by far too many young people leaving care. Opportunities for gradual transitions are best provided by placements where young people are settled and their carers are able to support them during transition into adulthood, or if that is not possible, by transitional or 'halfway' supportive arrangements.

Support after care

Young people leaving care, who are often estranged from their families, should be supported during their journey, well into adulthood – from ages 21 to 25 – not just at the time of leaving care. Research shows that there are considerable 'costs' in poor outcomes, both to young people themselves and to public services (Stein and Munro, 2008). There are different ways of providing support services.

In the UK, specialist leaving care schemes have developed to respond to the core needs of care leavers for assistance with accommodation, finance, education and careers, personal support networks and health and well-being. Each young person leaving care has a personal adviser or specialist worker who is responsible for carrying out a needs assessment and implementing a pathway plan. An important part of the work of specialist teams is the development of interagency links, to ensure an integrated approach to assisting young people with a range of different needs.

Outcome studies evaluating specialist leaving care services have shown that they can make a positive contribution to specific outcomes for care leavers. They work well in assisting young people in finding and settling in accommodation and in helping young people out of homelessness (Dixon and Stein, 2005). Research carried out in England provides evidence of the association between stability in accommodation after young people leave care and positive outcomes in terms of an enhanced sense of well-being, to some extent independent of young people's past care careers (Wade and Dixon, 2006; Dixon, 2008).

Leaving care services can also assist young people successfully with life skills and there is evidence from Scottish research of a significant association between preparation before leaving care and 'coping' after care (Dixon and Stein, 2005). Leaving care services can also help young people to some extent in furthering social networks, developing relationships and building self-esteem, although these dimensions are also closely connected with young people having positive, supportive informal relationships with family members or friends, or former foster carers.

Conclusion

The research findings discussed in this chapter have shown that young people leaving care, as a group, are likely to have a difficult transition to adulthood. For most, their journey may be shorter and more severe than that undertaken by most young people who have not been in care. The evidence suggests that although, as a group, these young people have a high risk of social exclusion, there are differences in their outcomes, between those who successfully 'move on', those who 'survive' and those who 'struggle'. These different transitions are associated with their pre-care experiences, the quality of care they receive, the nature of their transitions from care and the support they receive after they leave care, demanding a more comprehensive set of policies and practices across their lifecourse.

Key practice points
- Develop preventative services in order to provide support at home and avoid wherever possible young people going into care.
- Provide good-quality care that offers stability and continuity, a positive sense of identity and well-being, assistance to overcome educational deficits and holistic preparation for adulthood.
- Develop opportunities that allow gradual transitions from care rather than expecting an instant transfer to adulthood.
- Provide support over an extended period into adulthood rather than focusing support solely at the point of transition.
- Promote the development of specialist leaving care schemes, which provide a personal adviser or specialist worker for each young person leaving care.
- Support individuals to maintain stable accommodation in order to maximise the potential for good long-term outcomes.

References

Ajayi, S. and Quigley, M. (2006) 'By degrees: care leavers in higher education', in E. Chase, A. Simon and S. Jackson (eds) *In care and after, a positive perspective*, London: Routledge.

Barn, R., Andrew, L. and Mantovani, N. (2005) *Life after care: A study of young people from different ethnic groups*, York: Joseph Rowntree Foundation.

Berridge, D. (2007) 'Theory and explanation in child welfare; education and looked-after children', *Child and Family Social Work*, vol 12, no 1, pp 1-10.

Biehal, N. (2005) *Working with adolescents: Supporting families, preventing breakdown*, London: BAAF.

Biehal, N. and Wade, J. (1996) 'Looking back, looking forward: care leavers, families and change', *Children and Youth Services Review*, vol 18, no 4/5, pp 425-45.

Biehal, N., Clayden, J., Stein, M. and Wade, J. (1995) *Moving on: Young people and leaving care schemes*, London: HMSO.

Broad, B. (2005) *Improving the health and well being of young people leaving care*, Lyme Regis: Russell House Publishing.

Chase, E., Knight, A., Warwick, I. and Aggleton, P. *(2003) Pregnancy and parenthood among young people in and leaving local authority care*, Report for the Department of Health, London: Thomas Coram Research Unit.

Cheesebrough, S. (2002) The educational attainment of people who have been in care: Findings from the 1970 British Cohort Study, London: Social Exclusion Unit, www.socialexclusionunit.gov.uk.

Cheung, S.Y. and Buchanan, A. (1997) 'Malaise scores in adulthood of children and young people who have been in care', Journal of Child Psychology and Psychiatry, vol 38, no 5, pp 575-80.

Clayden, J. and Stein, M. (2005) *Mentoring young people leaving care: 'Someone for me'*, York: Joseph Rowntree Foundation.

Coleman, J.C. and Hendry, L. (1999) *The nature of adolescence*, London: Routledge.

Craig, T. (1996) Off to a bad start, London: Mental Health Foundation.

CSCI (Commission for Social Care Inspection) (2007) *Social Services Performance Assessment Framework indicators, children 2005-6*, London: CSCI.

DCSF (Department for Children, Schools and Families) (2007) Impact assessment for White Paper on children in care, London: DCSF.

DCSF (2008a) *Children looked after in England year ending March 2007*, London: DCSF.

DCSF (2008b) *Care matters: Time to deliver for Children in Care: An implementation plan*, London: DCSF.

DfES (Department for Education and Skills) (2001) *Youth Cohort Study: The activities and experiences of 21 year olds: England and Wales 2000*, London: DfES.

DHSSPS (NI) (Department for Health, Social Services and Public Safety (Northern Ireland) (2007) *Children in care statistics*, Belfast: DHSSPS (NI).

Dixon, J. (2008) 'Young people leaving care: health, well-being and outcomes', *Child and Family Social Work*, vol 13, no 2, pp 207-17.

Dixon, J. and Stein, M. (2005) *Leaving care, through care and aftercare in Scotland*, London: Jessica Kingsley Publishers.

DWP (Department for Work and Pensions) (2004) *Householders below average income: An analysis of the income distribution 1994/5-2002/3*, Leeds: Corporate Document Services.

Gibbs, I., Sinclair, I. and Stein, M. (2005) 'Children and young people in and leaving care', in J. Bradshaw and E. Mayhew (eds) *The well-being of children in the UK*, London: Save the Children.

Hart, A. (1984) 'Resources for transitions from care', in *Leaving care – where? Conference report*, London: National Association of Young People in Care.

Hobcraft, J. (1998) Intergenerational and life-course transmission of social exclusion: Influences of childhood poverty, family disruption and contact with the police, CASE Paper 15, London: London School of Economics and Political Science.

Hobcraft, J. and Kiernan, K. (1999) Childhood poverty, early motherhood and adult social exclusion, Case Paper 28, London: London School of Economics and Political Science.

Horrocks, C. (2002) 'Using life course theory to explore the social and developmental pathways of young people leaving care', Journal of Youth Studies, vol 5, no 3, pp 325-35.

Jackson, S. and Thomas, N. (2001) *What works in creating stability for looked after children*, Ilford: Barnardos.

Jones, G. (2002) *The youth divide*, York: Joseph Rowntree Foundation.

Koprowska, J. and Stein, M. (2000) 'The mental health of "looked after" young people', in P. Aggleton, J. Hurry and I. Warwick (eds) Young people and mental health, Chichester: Wiley.

Melzer, H., Corbin, T., Gatward, R., Goodman, R. and Ford, T. (2003) *The mental health of young people looked after by local authorities in England*, London: National Statistics.

NAW (National Assembly for Wales) (2007) *Social services statistics*, Cardiff: NAW.

Newburn, T., Ward, J. and Pearson, G. (2002) Drug use among young people in care, Research Briefing 7, Swindon: ESRC.

Priestley, M., Rabiee, P. and Harris, J. (2003) 'Young disabled people and the "new arrangements" for leaving care in England and Wales', *Children and Youth Services Review*, vol 25, no 11, pp 863-90.

Rabiee, P., Priestley, M. and Knowles, J. (2001) *Whatever next? Young disabled people leaving care*, Leeds: First Key.

Scottish Government (2007) *Children looked after statistics 2006-7*, Edinburgh: Scottish Government.

SEU (Social Exclusion Unit) (1998) *Rough sleeping*, London: The Stationery Office.

Sinclair, I., Baker, C., Wilson, K. and Gibbs, I. (2005) *Foster children, where they go and how they get on*, London: Jessica Kingsley Publishers.

Stein, M. (2004) *What works for young people leaving care?*, Barkingside: Barnardos.

Stein, M. (2005) *Resilience and young people leaving care*, York: Joseph Rowntree Foundation, www.jrf.org.uk/bookshop/details.asp?pubID=732

Stein, M. (2006) 'Young people aging out of care: the poverty of theory', *Children and Youth Services Review*, vol 28, no 3, pp 422-35.

Stein, M. and Munro, E. (eds) (2006) *Young people's transitions from care to adulthood: International research and practice*, London: Jessica Kingsley Publishers.

Wade, J. and Dixon, J. (2006) 'Making a home, finding a job: investigating early housing and employment outcomes for young people leaving care', *Child and Family Social Work*, vol 11, no 4, pp 199-208.

Wade, J., Mitchell, F. and Baylis, G. (2005) *Unaccompanied asylum seeking children: The response of social work services*, London: BAAF.

FOUR

Transitions for young people with learning disabilities

Gillian MacIntyre

Introduction

This chapter will explore the nature of transition from childhood to adulthood for one particularly vulnerable group of young people – those with learning disabilities. It will outline their experiences of transition before examining policy responses in relation to these experiences.

The process of transition has become increasingly complex for all young people. This can be ascribed to structural factors such as the collapse of the youth labour market, increased participation in further and higher education, changing family composition and a lack of affordable housing (Jones, 2002; Furlong et al, 2003). The transition from childhood to adulthood involves:

- leaving school and moving on to further education, training or employment;
- leaving the family home and moving to a home of one's own;
- leaving the family of origin and establishing a family of one's own.

When an individual has achieved these markers of adult status, they can be said to have made a successful transition to adulthood. Adulthood can be defined as:

> ... an emergent status realized through the gradual acquisition of certain rights, privileges and responsibilities ... such a natural progression cannot be taken for granted for young people with a learning disability. (May, 2000, p 27)

As the above quote suggests, for young people with learning disabilities the transitional process is likely to be even more problematic and young people face a number of difficulties. According to Hudson (2006), the transition to adulthood for young people with learning disabilities is wider in scope, of longer duration and is filled with attenuated experiences. These experiences threaten to slow down the transition or result in it not taking place at all.

The transition to adult status should not be confused with the transition from children's to adult services. Young people with learning disabilities can expect to make transitions that involve local education authorities, children's social services, adult social care and in some cases paediatric and adult health services. This transition is a complicated process that occurs at different ages and involves different eligibility criteria, depending on which organisations are involved.

Defining learning disability

There is currently no nationally agreed definition of what constitutes a 'learning disability' (Diesfield, 1999; Klotz, 2001; Ho, 2004). Moreover, the terminology used varies according to preferences: for example, 'learning disabilities', 'learning difficulties', 'intellectual disabilities'. The term 'learning disability' has been adopted here in order to maintain consistency with much of the British writing in the field. In addition, the majority of policy documents and service provision within the UK use the term 'learning disability' so using the term here avoids confusion. Some of the more medicalised definitions of learning disability continue to rely on IQ testing. Other definitions take a more functional approach, focusing on areas of difficulty in comparison with the general population. In 2002, the Department for Education and Skills (DfES, 2002, p 8) described moderate learning disability as:

> ... developmental delay across a number of areas. Pupils with moderate learning difficulty will have attainments below expected levels in most subjects in the curriculum. Pupils have difficulty in acquiring basic literacy and numeracy skills and in many cases will have speech and language difficulties associated with intellectual delay. A few may also have low self esteem, low levels of concentration, under-developed social skills and have behavioural, emotional and social difficulty and/or physical disability that affect their learning abilities.

In this chapter, it will be pointed out to the reader where possible whether the research refers to young people with moderate learning disabilities or to more severe or profound learning disabilities.

The experience of transition

The transition from childhood to adulthood can be regarded as a time of excitement and opportunity. For many young people, however, including those with learning disabilities, and their parents, it can often be a source of great anxiety. The fact that young people with learning disabilities experience difficult transitions in comparison with their non-disabled counterparts is not new. Research from the 1980s and early 1990s highlighted some of the difficulties faced. These early studies found that young disabled people were at a significant disadvantage in the labour market. Walker (1982) found that those young disabled people who did have employment tended to be concentrated in a narrow range of low-skilled jobs that were often insecure, repetitive and unrewarding, with poor conditions. Likewise, Anderson and Clarke (1982) highlighted the inadequate preparation that disabled young people were offered in the transition between school and work (see also Fish and McGinty, 1992). Young people in their study were much less likely than the general population to have a paid job, set up households of their own, marry or have a family.

Hirst and Baldwin (1994) found that disabled people were only half as likely to be in employment as a comparison group of non-disabled people. In addition, half of the disabled young people either attended day centres or had no formal weekday activities. They also found differences between disabled people with different kinds of impairments (see also Hirst, 1987; Clark and Hirst, 1989) with the most severely disabled being the most severely disadvantaged. Those disabled young people who did manage to attain paid work were most likely to be junior non-manual workers engaged in clerical and sales occupations (30%) or unskilled (19%) and semi-skilled (19%) manual workers in catering, cleaning or manufacturing (Hirst and Baldwin, 1994).

In recent years, a range of policy measures including the publication of *The same as you?* in Scotland (Scottish Executive, 2000), *Valuing people* in England (DH, 2001), *The equal lives report* in Northern Ireland (Northern Ireland Executive, 2005) and a *Statement on policy and practice for adults with learning disabilities* in Wales (WAG, 2007) resulted in changing expectations for people with learning disabilities at a number of levels. A range of initiatives such as the reconfiguration of local authority day services and the introduction of a range of measures to encourage disabled people into the labour market such as the New Deal for Disabled People meant that disabled people, their families, policy makers and practitioners expected more than life in an adult training centre. In Scotland, a short-term working group on employment (Scottish Executive, 2003, p 3) stated that 'people with learning disabilities have an expectation of employment. They no longer have just wishes and dreams'.

Indeed, the expectations of adult life of young people with learning disabilities are similar to those of young people in the general population. A study by Tarleton and Ward (2006) found that young people with learning disabilities expected to work, go to college, have a social life, continue their leisure pursuits, make friends and have relationships. It can be argued that young people with learning disabilities making the transition from childhood to adulthood in the early part of the 21st century make increasingly similar transitions to their non-disabled counterparts. This is not to suggest that transition to adulthood for this group has become unproblematic, as the remainder of the chapter shows.

The experience of further education for young people with disabilities

Although young people with learning disabilities have more choice now when leaving school than they did in the past, research that has explored the experiences of young adults with disabilities has highlighted that difficulties in making the transition from school to further education, training or employment persist. According to Mitchell (1999), post-school training has become a significant part of many disabled young people's lives, partly due to the expansion of further education (see also Riddell et al, 2001). Mitchell suggests that for those young people who had previously attended a special school, further education college provided an opportunity to move on to a more adult, mainstream environment. In reality, however, young people's experiences of college continued to be separately organised and managed. Often, there was little non-disabled peer interaction, and work experience (a key feature of many college courses) was not open to everyone (Mitchell, 1999). Wider socioeconomic factors such as work placements available and the support offered by employers were important excluding mechanisms. In addition, the opportunity structure was frequently mediated and interpreted by professional assessments and judgements of what was regarded as feasible (Mitchell, 1999).

These findings are supported by other research in this area. Riddell et al (2001) found that in two of the fieldwork areas studied, few choices were available to young people with learning disabilities. They were allocated college places rather than being able to choose from different options. The increasing marketisation of further education has targeted additional resources on those with special needs but this has not balanced out disadvantages suffered by people with disabilities in the labour market. If anything, the targeting of young people with learning disabilities further disadvantages them by labelling them as 'special' and removing them from the mainstream. Premium funding, which was provided for the education of students with additional support needs, has in some cases led to an increase in segregated provision (Watson et al, 2003). Riddell et al (2001) found that education tended to be in segregated settings allowing little contact with non-disabled peers. In addition, the absence of supported and open employment opportunities for young people with learning disabilities means that the most likely destination after college is an adult training centre, despite the policy rhetoric and changing expectations outlined above.

Similarly, Watson and Farmakopoulou (2003) found that despite the attempts of government policies for inclusive learning, the majority of provision for disabled students in colleges remained segregated. In addition, certain groups of students appeared to have been in the same class over several years or appeared to move from one segregated course to another within the same or different colleges. Such courses did not always lead to qualifications and the main benefits of college appeared to be social (Watson et al, 2003). Indeed, research by Pitt and Curtin (2004) found that for disabled students attending further education college, far from feeling socially segregated, it appeared that there were positive personal and social effects of being with similarly disabled people (these young people had previously reported experiences of bullying while attending mainstream school). The research suggests that the primary benefit of further education for disabled young people appears to be social and Watson et al (2003) suggest that the emphasis of further education should perhaps shift from human to social capital principles such as citizenship, capacity building and empowerment.

Despite the difficulties faced by young people with learning disabilities in terms of gaining qualifications or employability skills while at college, they continue to aspire to employment and, overall, have an optimistic and pragmatic view of the future (see Conners and Stalker, 2002). Recent research on the transitional experiences of young disabled people suggests that the transition to paid employment continues to be problematic.

Disabled young people's experiences of employment

Young people with learning disabilities continue to face a range of barriers in terms of finding and sustaining paid employment. In Wales, for example, the most recent figures suggest that between 10 and 17% of people with learning disabilities are in employment compared with 47% of the general disabled population (Beyer, 2008). Morris (2002), in a review of research on young disabled people's transitions, suggested that the variability of support services to assist young disabled people into employment, such as supported employment projects, is a significant factor. The availability of such projects varies locally and many projects are short term and insecure. In addition, specialist schools and colleges appear to lack information about such opportunities as they rarely refer young disabled people to supported employment agencies (Morris, 2002), the end result being that young disabled people are 'hurtling into a void' upon leaving school (Morris, 1999).

During transition planning, employment is not frequently considered as an option in its own right. Very few 16- to 19-year-olds enter supported employment upon leaving school (Beyer, 2008). Often, the attitudes and low expectations of disabled people, their families and various practitioners result in employment not being considered as a serious option, particularly for those with more significant impairments (Morris, 1999, 2002). A similar picture emerged for young disabled people making the transition from childhood to adulthood in Scotland (Stalker, 2002). The benefits system was identified as a significant barrier that can often deter young disabled people from looking for work or can lead their parents to discourage them from doing so. This is particularly the case when the young person's benefits makes up a substantial proportion of the household income (Weston, 2002).

These findings are supported by the work of Pascall and Hendey (2002, 2004) who examined the transitional experiences of young people with a range of disabilities in relation to both paid employment and independent living. They identified a range of barriers to paid employment for people with disabilities, including a lack of qualifications, employer attitudes and the benefits system. They also pointed out that young people with disabilities found it extremely difficult to achieve both paid employment and independent living. The benefits system had a crucial role to play and respondents in their study felt that the benefits system was often at the heart of their difficulties in combining different aspects of adult status (Pascall and Hendey, 2002). The type of work available meant that young people were unlikely to earn enough to pay for accommodation and personal assistance costs, making benefits an attractive option in this respect. Those young people who were able to combine different aspects of adult status were likely to have 'exceptional parents' (Pascall and Hendey, 2004) who were likely to be in higher occupational categories with social, cultural and economic resources to assist their child make a prolonged transition to adulthood.

Transition and choice

It would appear that young people with learning disabilities making the transition from childhood to adulthood face similar issues to young people in the general population. Globalisation has changed the nature of employment (see Jolly, 2000; Roulstone, 2002). Workers are entering an increasingly risk-based employment domain where the type of work available is short term and part time, with a growth in self-employment. The labour market is increasingly flexible and although this might bring some advantages to disabled workers in terms, for example, of ability to adapt working hours, it is likely that increasingly flexibility within the labour market will actually result in employees having to satisfy increasingly stringent criteria to retain employment (Jolly, 2000). Declining employment opportunities for young people generally have occurred at a time when there is a growing expectation of participation in the labour market for people with disabilities. Young people in the general population have adopted an 'unsettled life' through choice. This involves continuing in education, travelling and denial of interest in long-term relationships, marriage and parenting (Caton and Kagan, 2007).

Disabled young people are less able to exercise such choices. Bignall et al (2002) argue that although there has been a great deal of rhetoric about opening up choices to young disabled people, in practice the structures of education and training channel them down particular routes, which may not reflect their own aspirations. Findings of a national study conducted between 2004 and 2007 by Beyer found a clear bias towards moving young people with learning disabilities on to further education college. Indeed, 60% of those carers questioned reported that schools had failed to mention employment as an option (Beyer, 2008). Similarly, a study by MacIntyre (2007, 2008) found that 18 of 20 young people with learning disabilities who participated in the research moved on to further education after leaving school. Two years later, six of the young people were still in further education, four were on a training programme, seven were economically inactive and three had paid employment.

MacIntyre (2007) found that although people with learning disabilities experienced an increasing range of options in relation to education, training and employment, they remained in a marginalised position, similar to that of other groups of disadvantaged people. They were more likely, for example, to be overrepresented in the group of young people who are not in education, employment or training. Although all young people are experiencing extended transitions with a range of choices and opportunities, the actual experiences of that delayed transition are very different. For young people with learning disabilities, the transitional experience is likely to be less fulfilling and less optimistic (Caton and Hagan, 2007). In reality, young people with learning disabilities are likely to face social isolation at the time of transition. The extended periods that they are likely to spend in education or training are often viewed negatively and there are less opportunities to make decisions or take risks. Parents are often anxious to minimise risk and activities such as accessing money and choosing friends are areas where they feel it is legitimate to intervene (Shepperdson, 2001, quoted in Hudson, 2003).

Young people with profound and complex needs

It is unsurprising that these negative experiences are further exacerbated for young people with more severe or profound learning disabilities. For this group of young people, leaving home is likely to take place later and young people will not gain legal independence if they are not deemed as having capacity. They are also unlikely to have an independent social life as a result of a lack of accessible transport, communication issues, adult surveillance and lack of access to a peer group. People with more severe learning disabilities continue to be one of the most marginalised groups in society. A survey conducted by the Department of Health in 2005 found that of 3,000 people with learning disabilities, 32% said that someone had been rude or offensive to them in the previous year. In addition, 31% had no contact with friends (DH, 2005).

For those young people in out-of-area placements, the transition to adulthood continues to be problematic. Heslop et al (2007) highlighted a number of problems with the transition process for this group of young people. In general terms and in common with the experiences outlined above, there appeared to be a lack of information for parents, young people and professionals about the different alternatives available and the process was perceived to start too late. Problems were exacerbated for this particular group of young people because of the geographical distance involved. There were issues around professionals refusing to travel to meetings and a number of complications with regard to funding. Overall, parents found the process of transition to be difficult and stressful. The young people in Heslop's study had 'little or no sense of future progression ... there was a considerable lack of expectations about their futures' (Heslop et al, 2007, p vii).

Policy responses

This chapter has outlined in detail the experience of transition for young people with a range of learning disabilities. It is clear that they face a number of difficulties – some of which are similar to young people in the general population and some that are particular to their experience of being a young person with a learning disability. These difficulties have been recognised by policy makers and have been incorporated into a number of different policy documents. In 2001, objective 2 of *Valuing people* (DH, 2001, p 1) stated services must ensure that:

> ... as young people with learning disabilities move into adulthood to ensure continuity of care and support for the young person and their family and to provide equality of opportunity in order to enable as many disabled people as possible to participate in education, training or employment.

Similarly, the *National Service Framework for Children, Young People and Maternity Services* (DH, 2004) pointed out that disabled young people should have good-quality, multiagency support to enable them to make choices and have control over their own lives. To this end, a number of changes were introduced. These included:

- the introduction of Learning Disability Partnership Boards in all local authorities in October 2001. These boards are responsible for adult learning disability services and it was envisaged that they would ensure that arrangements were in place to enable a smooth transition to adult life for young people;
- the establishment of the Learning Disability Development Fund, which provides money to each Partnership Board to, among other things, support advocacy and person-centred planning;
- the establishment of the Connexions service. This service offers support to all young people at the time of transition but targets those who need it most. Its main remit is to support existing

agencies rather than providing something new or different. Connexions can offer support to young people up to the age of 25;

• the establishment of Inclusiveness projects in Scotland, with key workers whose remit was to support young people with additional support needs to make the transition from childhood to adulthood. These projects had a particular focus on improving young people's employability (MacIntyre, 2007, 2008).

In recognition of the need for good information at transition, a transition information network was established in order to disseminate important information about transition. The Department for Education and Skills (now the Department for Children, Schools and Families) was responsible for producing advice for young people with learning disabilities making the transition from school. This advice was to be disseminated by the information network (DH, 2005).

Despite these measures and a plethora of good practice guidelines such as *Aiming high for disabled children: Better support to families* (DfES, 2007), *A transition guide for all services* (DCSF, 2008) and *Transition: Moving on well* (DH, 2008), the Government recognised that implementation of transition planning had been patchy and inconsistent. In the consultation paper *Valuing people now: From progress to implementation* (DH, 2007), transition from childhood to adulthood remained a high priority:

> Young people in transition should always be a focus and target for early action when developing strategies to support people into paid work, access ordinary housing, introduce individual budgets and undertake comprehensive health checks. (DH, 2007, p 32)

In England it is anticipated that in the next three years, every young person with learning disabilities will have person-centred reviews from the age of 14 to 19, based on a person-centred plan that will be written in Year 9 of school. It is also envisaged that greater numbers of younger people with learning disabilities will move into employment and will take up Individual Budgets and Direct Payments. A Transition Support Programme, which represents an investment of £19 million, has been established. Part of this money will be used to promote these person-centred approaches to transition. All young people with learning disabilities will be provided with an information pack and will have access to an adviser and advocacy service. In addition, the Getting a

Life Programme will bring together funding and assessment systems for young people going through transition, with the aim of getting a job, an education and a social life (DH, 2007). In order to ensure progress, Public Service Agreement 12 commits the Department of Health and the Department for Children, Schools and Families to establish a Transitions Support Programme and to develop a Transition Planning Tool (Liveability, 2008). Similar initiatives are under way in the rest of the UK.

Effectiveness

The impact of these new measures remains to be seen. However, a number of examples of good practice have been identified (CSCI, 2007). These include:

- transition personal advisers based in learning disability teams;
- initiatives developed in partnership with families, local authorities, primary care teams and local universities to bring young people back to their communities from out-of-area placements;
- better use of information technology to track the number of people receiving a service before transition, their current services and any reasons for changes;
- transition planning panels to capture data about young people and to monitor the quality of transition plans;
- proactive planning with housing partners to ensure that supported accommodation is available.

Despite these illustrations of good practice, progress has been patchy. Hudson (2006) has suggested that a lack of resources and clear targets up until this point has not been helpful in terms of moving things forward. The research evidence throughout this chapter illustrates the difficulties that young people making transitions continue to face. It would appear that planning for transition still occurs too late and the information needs of parents and young people remain unmet (Tarleton and Ward, 2005). The separation of children's services and adult social care has complicated the matter further and there is a lack of clarity with regard to who should take responsibility for transitions. Different agencies take responsibility for children and young people at different ages and stages and this can create further confusion. In addition, different levels of eligibility criteria and different levels of funding available for children's and adults' services mean that the level and type of services available at transition are likely to change (CSCI,

2007). Further financial and organisational pressures relate to National Health Service (NHS) continuing care criteria, which are not consistent across children's and adults' services, and the loss of ringfenced funding for Supporting People. Joint working and joint commissioning have yet to reach their full potential in this area and the research evidence suggests that not all professionals are fully engaged in the process. In Scotland, for example, the introduction of the 2005 Education (Additional Support for Learning) (Scotland) Act has resulted in less involvement in transitional planning from social workers and health professionals. This can be explained in part by the fact that the statutory duty for transition planning lies with education authorities only (Kane and MacIntyre, 2009). Similar difficulties with engagement exist across the rest of the UK.

There is some hope for optimism, however, with greater use being made of person-centred plans and the increased use of self-directed support alongside the introduction of Individualised Budgets. These offer an important means of achieving normal life opportunities for young people with learning disabilities. Yet shifting the balance of control to young people and their families will only be effective if appropriate planning measures and services are available. Local commissioners will have an important role to play in terms of ensuring that the full range of services needed by young people with learning disabilities is available (Liveability, 2008).

Conclusions and recommendations

This chapter has highlighted the increased priority given to the transition from childhood to adulthood for young people with learning disabilities. Clearly, a significant amount of progress has been achieved in the last 30 years. This progress relates particularly to the expectations of young people, their families and the professionals who work with them. They are increasingly demanding the same opportunities as other young people and will no longer settle for life in a day centre. They expect to be able to further their education, live independently, find paid work and make new relationships. Policy documents such as *The same as you* (Scottish Executive, 2000) and *Valuing people* (DH, 2001) have encouraged these aspirations.

While it is clear that many more opportunities are available than previously, the research evidence presented in this chapter suggests that for many young people with learning disabilities the outcomes continue to be unsatisfactory. Young people with learning disabilities continue to be overrepresented in the group of young people who are not in education, employment or training. In addition, they are less likely to live independently. A study of 3,000 adults with learning disabilities in 2005 found that 51% continued to live with their parents (DH, 2005). Young people with learning disabilities are also likely to be socially isolated despite having greater access to mainstream opportunities.

The result has been to emphasise the need to listen to what young people really want at the point of transition via the mechanism of person-centred planning. While this is commendable, the process of transition planning continues to be flawed. All too often, young people and their families continue to experience delays and confusion, with accessible information remaining a significant problem.

The challenge for the government therefore remains – to close the gap between national policy and local implementation. There is a need to involve young people and their families more meaningfully in the transition process. This entails listening to what young people want and empowering them to make choices while at the same time acknowledging that the notion of choice can be very difficult for some young people, who might not have had the opportunity to make decisions about their own life in the past.

It is also important but extremely difficult to acknowledge that current policies of inclusion create tension for young people with the most severe learning disabilities. This is not to advocate a return to policies of segregation, but to acknowledge that for some young people a more meaningful transition plan might focus on building and establishing meaningful relationships and community links rather than emphasising employment. Clegg and colleagues (2008) suggest that this focus on employment and individual attainment is a result of political rhetoric and moral pressures and judgements. They suggest that:

> Difficulties encountered over inclusion at transition are unlikely to be resolved by doing more of the same … there is a need to address service gaps but also acknowledge the moral pressures and judgements that complicate decision-making and to shift the moral compass away from individual achievement and towards engagement and relationships. (Clegg et al, 2008, p 93)

This chapter suggests that there is some cause for optimism. The increased focus on the individual and careful planning should result in more positive outcomes for young people with learning disabilities. Finally, the overall goal of transition planning should be reiterated.

Ultimately, the transition process is not about getting someone services, it is about getting someone a life (Dimensions, 2007).

Key practice points

- There needs to be greater use of person-centred planning to ensure that young people with learning disabilities experience a transition process that is unique to them and their goals.
- Young people and their families should be involved more meaningfully in the transition process. Their wants and goals should be listened to and then a plan should be created to make these happen rather than simply providing a list of options.
- All post-school options should be considered. At present there is evidence of young people being channelled down the further education route. This is not the best option for every young person.
- Clear protocols for joint working need to be established that highlight roles and responsibilities for different aspects of the transition process.
- Planning for transition must take place earlier to ensure that all necessary components are in place to support young people when they leave school.
- Better data collection tools must be introduced to ensure that an accurate record of young people about to undertake transition is available for relevant agencies.

References

Anderson, E.M. and Clarke, L. (1982) *Disability in adolescence*, London: Methuen.

Beyer, S. (2008) *Transition from school to employment: What works?*, Wales: Llais.

Bignall, T., Butt, J. and Pagarani, D. (2002) *'Something to do': The development of peer support groups for young black and minority ethnic disabled and Deaf people*, Bristol/York: The Policy Press/Joseph Rowntree Foundation.

Caton, S. and Kagan, C. (2007) 'Comparing transition experiences of young people with moderate learning disabilities with other vulnerable youth and their non-disabled counterparts', *Disability and Society*, vol 22, no 5, pp 473-88.

Clark, A. and Hirst, M. (1989) 'Disability in adulthood: ten year follow up study of young people with disabilities', *Disability, Handicap and Society*, vol 4, pp 271-83.

Clegg, J., Murphy, E., Almack, K. and Harvey, A. (2008) 'Tensions around inclusion: reframing the moral horizon', *Journal of Applied Research on Intellectual Disabilities*, vol 21, no 1, pp 81-94.

Conners, C. and Stalker, K. (2002) *The views and experiences of disabled children and their siblings: A positive outlook*, London: Jessica Kingsley Publishers.

CSCI (Commission for Social Care Inspection) (2007) *Growing up matters: Better transition planning for young people with complex needs*, London: CSCI.

DCSF (Department for Children, Schools and Families) (2008) *A transition guide for all services: Key information for professionals about the transition process for disabled young people*, Nottingham: DCSF.

DfES (Department for Education and Skills) (2002) *Classification of special educational needs: Consultation document*, London: DfES, www.dfes.gov.uk/sen

DfES (2007) *Aiming high for disabled children: Better support to families*, London: DfES.

DH (Department of Health) (2001) *Valuing people: A new strategy for learning disability for the 21st century*, London: HMSO.

DH (2004) *National Service Framework for Children, Young People and Maternity Services*, London: HMSO.

DH (2005) *The government's annual report on learning disability 2005*, London: HMSO.

DH (2007) *Valuing people now: From progress to transformation*, London: DH.

DH (2008) *Transition: Moving on well: A good practice guide for health professionals and their partners on transition planning for young people with complex health needs or a disability*, London: DH.

Diesfield, K. (1999) 'International ethical safeguards: genetics and people with learning disabilities', *Disability and Society*, vol 14, no 1, pp 21-36.

Dimensions (2007) *Transition? How to find your way through: An overview of recent transitions research for parents and practitioners*, Theale: Dimensions.

Fish, J. and McGinty, J. (1992) *Learning and support for young people in transition: Leaving school for further education and work*, Buckingham: Open University Press.

Furlong, A., Cartmel, F., Biggart, A., Sweeting, H. and West, P. (2003) *Youth transitions: Patterns of vulnerability and processes of social inclusion*, Edinburgh: The Stationery Office.

Heslop, P., Abbott, D., Johnson, L. and Mallett, R. (2007) *Help to move on*, York: York Publishing Services.

Hirst, M. (1987) 'Patterns of impairment and disability related to social handicap in young people with cerebral palsy', *Journal of Biosocial Science*, vol 21, no 1, pp 1-12.

Hirst, M. and Baldwin, S. (1994) *Unequal opportunities: Growing up disabled*, London: Social Policy Research Unit.

Ho, A. (2004) 'To be labelled or not to be labelled: that is the question', *British Journal of Learning Disabilities*, vol 32, no 1, pp 86-92.

Hudson, B. (2003) 'From adolescence to young adulthood: the partnership challenge for learning disability services in England', *Disability and Society*, vol 18, no 3, pp 259-76.

Hudson, B. (2006) 'Making and missing connections: learning disability services and the transition from adolescence to adulthood', *Disability and Society*, vol 21, no 1, pp 47-60.

Jolly, D. (2000) 'A critical evaluation of the contradictions for the disabled worker arising from the emergence of the flexible labour market in Britain', *Disability and Society*, vol 15, no 5, pp 795-810.

Jones, G. (2002) *The youth divide: Diverging paths to adulthood*, York: Joseph Rowntree Foundation.

Kane, J. and MacIntyre, G. (2009) *Post-school transitions for young people with additional support needs*, Final report to the Esmee Fairbairn Foundation, Glasgow: University of Glasgow.

Klotz, J. (2001) 'Sociocultural study of intellectual disability: moving beyond labelling and social constructionist perspectives', *British Journal of Learning Disabilities*, vol 32, no 2, pp 93-104.

Liveability (2008) *Freedom to live: Transition for disabled young people: Liveability's report on disabled young people moving towards adulthood*, Bedford: NewNorth Print.

MacIntyre, G. (2007) 'What next? Opportunities for young people with learning disabilities after leaving school', Unpublished PhD thesis, University of Glasgow.

MacIntyre, G. (2008) *Learning disability and social inclusion*, Edinburgh: Dunedin Academic Press.

May, D. (2000) 'Becoming adult: school leaving, jobs and the transition to adult life', in D. May (ed) *Transition and change in the lives of people with intellectual disabilities*, London: Jessica Kingsley Publishers.

Mitchell, W. (1999) 'Leaving special school: the next step and future aspirations', *Disability and Society*, vol 14, no 3, pp 753-69.

Morris, J. (1999) *Hurtling into a void: Transition to adulthood for young people with complex health and support needs*, Brighton: Pavilion Publishing.

Morris, J. (2002) *Moving into adulthood: Young disabled people moving into adulthood*, York: Joseph Rowntree Foundation.

Northern Ireland Executive (2005) *The equal lives report*, Belfast: Northern Ireland Executive.

Pascall, G. and Hendey, N. (2002) *Disability and transition to adulthood: Achieving independent living*, Bristol: Pavilion Publishing

Pascall, G. and Hendey, N. (2004) 'Disability and transition to adulthood: the politics of parenting', *Critical Social Policy*, vol 24, no 2, pp 165-85.

Pitt, V. and Curtin, M. (2004) 'Integration v segregation: the experiences of a group of disabled students moving from mainstream school into special needs further education', *Disability and Society*, vol 19, no 4, pp 352-61.

Riddell, S., Baron, S. and Wilson, A. (2001) *The learning society and people with learning difficulties*, Bristol: The Policy Press.

Roulstone, A. (2002) 'Disabling pasts, enabling futures? How does the changing nature of capitalism impact on the disabled worker and job-seeker?', *Disability and Society*, vol 17, no 6, pp 627-42.

Scottish Executive (2000) *The same as you? Review of learning disability services in Scotland*, Edinburgh: The Stationery Office.

Scottish Executive (2003) *Working for a change? Report of the short life working group on employment. Same as you? National implementation team*, Edinburgh: The Stationery Office.

Stalker, K. (2002) *Young disabled people moving into adulthood in Scotland*, York: Joseph Rowntree Foundation.

Tarleton, B. and Ward, L. (2005) 'Changes and choices: finding out what information young people with learning disabilities, their parents and supporters need at transition', *British Journal of Learning Disabilities*, vol 33, no 1, pp 70-6.

WAG (Welsh Assembly Government) (2007) *Statement on policy and practice for adults with a learning disability*, Cardiff: WAG.

Walker, A. (1982) *Unqualified and underemployed: Handicapped young people and the labour market*, London: Macmillan.

Watson, N. and Farmakopoulou, N. (2003) 'Motivations for entering and pathways of progression of disabled students in further education', *International Journal of Inclusive Education*, vol 7, no 3, pp 223-39.

Watson, N., McKie, L., Hughes, B., Hopkins, D. and Gregory, S. (2003) '(Inter)dependence, needs and care: the potential for disability and feminist theorists to develop an emancipatory model', *Sociology*, vol 38, no 2, pp 331-50.

Weston, J. (2002) Choosing, getting and keeping a job: A study of supported employment for people with complex needs, Edinburgh: Scottish Human Services Trust.

FIVE

Young people with mental health problems

Sarah Judd

Introduction

The transition from childhood to adulthood is an uncertain time for all young people, but many also experience mental health difficulties. It is estimated that up to 20% of 16- to 24-year-olds have a mental health issue at any one time (Singleton and Lewis, 2003). The majority of these will be young people experiencing anxiety or depression, although other mental health conditions, such as schizophrenia, are known to emerge in late adolescence (Ryan, 2006).

Young adults face a number of stressful transitions that can prove a trigger point for their mental health, including the transition from school to work or university, leaving the family home or managing relationships. As mentioned in earlier chapters, young people in higher education experience an extended adolescence, particularly if they remain in the family home while completing their studies or return home after university. This can involve an element of backtracking in which young adults revert to a form of dependence on their parents, a situation that is at odds with the linear conceptualisation of transition between Child and Adolescent Mental Health Services (CAMHS) and Adult Mental Health Services (AMHS) (Health and Social Care Advisory Service, 2006). It is therefore important that issues related to transition are acknowledged well after the young person has entered adult services.

This chapter looks at positive ways to improve transitional mental health services for young people aged between 16 and 24, while acknowledging the financial constraints on the sector as a whole. Rather than see transition as an event, it is important to acknowledge it as a process that takes place over a number of years to account for this extended period of instability for young adults (Health and Social Care Advisory Service, 2006). By listening to young people and encouraging a person-centred approach, services can be developed to ensure useful and effective provision. The joint working agenda needs to be applied to this situation to encourage greater collaboration between children's and adults' mental health services. Many young people arrive in mental health services with a complex range of other issues. A holistic approach that looks at wider problems may help them to engage with a range of services and ease their transition out of CAMHS.

Barriers to young adult engagement with mental health services

Poor-quality experiences of services at this stage can leave young adults disillusioned with mental health services, and affect their future take-up of adult services (DH, 2008). Service provision for young people aged between 16 and 18 varies across the UK. Some local authorities provide CAMHS until the age of 18, some only until the young person is 16, and others up to 18 only if the young person is in full-time education (Smith and Leon, 2001). This is particularly problematic if AMHS do not accept young people under 18, and it leaves the most vulnerable young people (those not in education) without support. As a result, not only is there a lack of specialist provision for young people aged 16-24, but in some areas young people can easily fall through the net at an age when they are most vulnerable.

There are innate differences in service provision and availability between CAMHS and AMHS. CAMHS is characterised by a developmental approach involving a much lower threshold of intervention than AMHS, which deals with more severe and long-term mental health problems. Few health professionals working in adult services have experience of working with young adults, and may not recognise conditions such as attention deficit hyperactivity disorder (ADHD), resulting in multiple referrals from CAMHS to other agencies (Richards and Vostanis, 2004; SEU, 2005b). Many vulnerable CAMHS service users therefore find themselves ineligible for AMHS, and lose support from mental health services altogether.

CAMHS four-tier strategic framework

CAMHS is split into four tiers and involves professionals from a variety of backgrounds including teachers, general practitioners and health visitors. Tier 1 provides a primary level of care by professionals working in universal services who can identify early signs of mental health problems and offer general advice. Tier 2 is provided by professionals working with those in universal services, such as paediatricians, educational psychologists and child and adolescent mental health workers. These professionals can provide training for other staff, outreach and assessment. Tiers 3 and 4 offer more specialised services for more complex and persistent disorders (DH, 2007). As AMHS has a higher entry threshold than CAMHS, many young people who received treatment at Tiers 1 and 2 do not receive adequate support as they make the transition into adulthood.

While research suggests that early intervention is key to helping young adults with mental health problems, many do not approach these services until they have a crisis, particularly if they have had negative or disrupted experiences with school or with children's services (SEU, 2005a). There tends to be a stigma attached to services with the term 'mental' in the title, and many young people do not want to be associated with a group labelled in this way (Richards and Vostanis, 2004). There has also been a lack of communication with black and minority ethnic communities to enable them to have an accurate understanding, awareness and perception of mental health services (Ryan, 2006). More needs to be done to ensure that young adults from such backgrounds engage with mental health services before they reach a crisis point.

Geography can also be a major issue that prevents a significant number of young adults with mental health problems from accessing services. Rural areas tend to be poorly served in terms of mental health services for children and young people as a whole, let alone in providing specialist services for young adults. Even if such services are available in nearby towns, it is often very difficult for young adults without independent transport to access them during opening hours (Howarth and Street, 2000).

Of increasing concern is the significant numbers of young people being placed on wards that are inappropriate to their age and needs. It is estimated that there are between 500 and 600 inappropriate admissions of young people per year on adult psychiatric wards, and between 150 and 200 admissions per year on paediatric wards (Smith and Leon, 2001). A 2004 report found that few AMHS staff had training or experience in working with young adults, child protection issues were not always addressed properly and there was a lack of provision of education and appropriate recreational facilities (Mental Health Act Commission, 2004). In another report, some young people were unable to maintain effective contact with family and friends, due either to distance or to adult ward policies banning under 18s from visiting the wards. Many felt that there was a lack of information available to them – service users and their families did not know what to expect on admission to an adult ward, and when they were going to be discharged (Office of the Children's Commissioner, 2007).

Early intervention

Early intervention has become common in government discourses across the UK, and is key to ensuring that young people are not left unsupported as they reach late adolescence and early adulthood, particularly in terms of mental health (NAW, 2001; OFMDFM, 2006; DCSF, 2007). The development of early intervention teams is crucial to the successful treatment of psychosis, a disorder that tends to emerge in late adolescence. Many of these teams are deliberately set up to work with young people aged between 14 and 35 (Johnson, 2003).

It is important that practitioners working with young people are aware of the importance of early intervention teams in promoting recovery and supporting transition for young people experiencing psychosis. Recognising this need, the Sainsbury Centre for Mental Health, along with colleagues from the Early Psychosis Prevention and Intervention Centre in Melbourne, the Initiative to Reduce the Impact of Schizophrenia in Birmingham and the Lambeth Early Onset Services in London, developed a 10-week training course, with sessions led by service users, carers and clinicians. Participants came from a variety of agencies including both child and adult mental health services, crisis intervention teams, and newly established early intervention teams. The course provided a forum for practitioners from different disciplines to develop new approaches and discuss key issues of early intervention (Johnson, 2003).

Joint working and improvements at a service level

Poor communication between agencies can lead to misunderstandings about the roles of different services, which will have a negative impact on the support available to young adults transferring from CAMHS to AMHS (Svanberg and Street, 2003). Structural changes in children's services have led to an increased focus on professionals from social care, education and health working together in multiagency teams to improve outcomes for service users. This is particularly prevalent for easing transitions for looked-after young people with mental health problems. As Stein states in Chapter Three, looked-after young people are more likely to experience an accelerated transition with little option of returning when leaving care becomes problematic. They are also more likely to experience the risk factors associated with mental health problems. McAuley and Young (2006) highlight the need for services to be multidisciplinary so that expertise from general practitioners and colleagues in education and special education can be drawn upon.

In the case of mental health transitions, however, this model of integrated working should be extended in a 'vertical' direction to encourage joint working between CAMHS and AMHS. Pooled budgets and joint commissioning could contribute to a smoother transition between services, while joint training of staff from both adults' and children's services could enable professionals to learn similar methods and share expertise so that all are trained to work with vulnerable young adults. The final report of the Scottish Needs Assessment Programme suggests using informal 'consultation' sessions alongside training to encourage colleagues from different agencies to meet and discuss mutual issues around mental health (Public Health Institute of Scotland, 2003). This is a cost-effective way of learning, and contributes to a wider culture of information-sharing and joint working that can influence the whole organisation. Devising protocols and using compatible systems would ensure that information is shared effectively between services and successfully communicated to the service users.

Forbes et al (2001) developed a conceptual framework for continuity of care that can be applied to demonstrate the different levels of continuity needed to support a young person through transition into AMHS:

- *experienced continuity* – the experience of a coordinated and smooth progression from the service user's point of view;
- *continuity of information* – excellent information transfer following the service user;
- cross-boundary and team continuity – effective communication between professionals and services with service users;
- flexible continuity – flexibility to the needs of the individual over time;
- longitudinal continuity – care from as few professionals as possible, consistent with other needs;

> • relational or personal continuity – one or more named individual professional(s) with whom the service user can establish and maintain a therapeutic relationship.

Most local service providers would be unable to fund an effective designated mental health service for young adults due to the volume of referrals from both children's and adults' services (Richards and Vostanis, 2004). However, they could train staff to work specifically with young people, so that there would be some practitioners working in mental health services with knowledge of the needs of this group. This would help to bridge the gap for these vulnerable young adults moving into AMHS, raise the profile of the needs of this group and allow greater cooperation and joint working between children's and adults' mental health services.

There is significant evidence to suggest that young offenders have more mental health problems than those who do not offend, so need more support in the transitions both out of prison and into adulthood (Kurtz et al, 1998; Carswell et al, 2004). However, a report published in 2002 showed that 35% of CAMHS have no joint working with youth justice services, and only 27% had made formal contact with them (Revolving Doors Agency, 2002). The support provided for young people with mental health problems after they have been released from secure units is significant because it helps to provide a model for positive relationships, and reinforces skills in a new context (Abrams et al, 2008). These young adults with multiple needs will experience multiple transitions, so a variety of agencies need to work together to achieve positive outcomes for this vulnerable group. How these transitions are managed will have a significant impact on the young person's engagement with adult services.

One model that could be used in mental health service development is the creation of a multiagency, multidisciplinary Joint Services Planning Group designed to coordinate and oversee development. This would include professionals from CAMHS and AMHS, psychologists, children's services, adults' services, Youth Offending Teams, Principal Youth Officers, the Probation Service, schools and voluntary sector youth projects. It could also include service commissioners from relevant health and local authority agencies (Smith and Leon, 2001). The Welsh strategy document *Everybody's business* emphasises the need for greater involvement of schools in young people's mental health, and the importance of ensuring that the role of Tier 1 services is sufficiently developed, possibly through training from Tier 2 professionals (Pithouse,

2002). Such joint working would not only coordinate the transition between CAMHS and AMHS, but also introduce all young people to a range of services that could support them after transition.

Non-statutory services are often seen as less stigmatising, and are more likely to work with young adults specifically as they do not have the age limit that CAMHS does (Smith and Leon, 2001; Richards and Vostanis, 2004). However, there is little stable, long-term funding for many voluntary sector mental health projects, and voluntary sector services working specifically with young people also struggle. Like statutory services, young adults are a low-priority group among voluntary sector organisations that offer support to adults as a whole (Howarth and Street, 2000). A sharing of expertise and pooled budgets between statutory and non-statutory organisations could provide a great improvement in services working with this age group in particular, and increase stability in transition for young adults.

Working with young people and families

As well as improvements at a service level, there are a number of ways in which practitioners can improve the way they work with young people and their families to help to ease the transition from CAMHS. One of the main barriers to this is the lack of information provided. There should be shared decision making between the young people, their families and practitioners about how the process of transition will work for them. Indeed, the importance of involving young people in planning processes and providing adequate information is acknowledged in both the *National service framework for children young people and maternity services* (DH, 2007) and the Scottish *Framework for promotion, prevention and care* (Scottish Executive, 2005).

A good example of this is the Brookside Unit in Essex, which works with young people with psychosis. Recognising a need for more proactive engagement, staff set up a psycho-educational group for up to eight young people aged 18–30 to facilitate transition to adult services. The group is known as Exchange, and provides ideas, information and support as a two-way process. It meets weekly for an hour and a half for 10 weeks at a local adult services centre, and introduces young people to facilities that may interest them, including an internet café and a sports club (Johnson, 2003). This means that the young people are already aware of the facilities available to them before they move up into adult services, but keep the safety net of familiar support for these 10 weeks to prevent them from falling out of the system.

The effectiveness of services for these young people, like any services, depends on how they are delivered. Young people emphasised the importance of staff showing respect, encouraging participation through discussion, and responding to issues that are causing concern to help them through the transitional process (Ryan, 2006). Transition will be more effective if professionals can build on what is stable in the service user's life, especially in terms of those who are providing support for the young person outside of mental health services, such as family and friends (Health and Social Care Advisory Service, 2006). It is also beneficial for young adults to talk to others who have been in a similar situation. A report by the Mental Health Foundation acknowledged that while counselling was helpful, it did not have to be with a trained counsellor. Key workers or other young people who had experienced transition into AMHS were also found to be beneficial (Smith and Leon, 2001).

Person-centred planning emphasises the needs of the individual young adult to smooth the transition to adult services. The Welsh strategy document *Everybody's business* (NAW, 2001) highlighted as its first objective the importance of establishing child-centred mental health services and involving parents and carers in the planning and commissioning of services. Individual key workers or mentors from children's services, especially someone who has built up a strong relationship with the young person, are crucial in helping young adults to make the transition out of CAMHS, providing the relational or personal continuity emphasised by Forbes et al (2001). By acting as a broker for the service user, they can develop relationships with local services and help to introduce young people to the specialist provision relevant to their needs (SEU, 2005a).

Many studies have shown that young people want to be involved in service development (Buston, 2002; Aubrey and Dahl, 2006). Young adults receiving mental healthcare not only wanted professionals to listen to them and treat them with respect, but also wanted to be involved in the actual running of the service, including recruitment and leading a support group to discuss issues and suggestions (Smith and Leon, 2001). It is important to provide services that fit in with the lives of the young adults being targeted. Long waiting lists may result in young people becoming disengaged with all mental health services, so the opportunity for intervention may be lost (Smith and Leon, 2001). Services need to be available at evenings and weekends, to fit around school or work. This fits in with a wider research emphasis on listening to service users and using their ideas in service development.

As mentioned earlier, the lack of communication with black and minority ethnic groups means that they often have a negative perception of how mental health services work with young people. However, professionals can work to break down some of these barriers, for example by holding meetings in the family's home, so that the young adult and their family do not feel threatened. The former Care Services Improvement Partnership (CSIP, 2007) suggested that practitioners should hold meetings in the family's first language and then translate into English if necessary, rather than the other way round. Again, this helps to encourage understanding about the positive work that mental health services are involved in, and prevent the family feeling threatened and excluded from discussions.

Holistic approach

Transition between adolescence and young adulthood is a process in which many aspects of life are changing simultaneously, often in contradictory ways. Both the Ten Year Strategy for Children and Young People (OFMDFM, 2006) and the Bamford Review of Mental Health and Learning Disability (2007) in Northern Ireland emphasised the importance of a 'whole-child' approach, particularly in transition, to reflect the complex nature of young people's lives. According to a Social Exclusion Unit questionnaire, 98% of young adults accessing services had more than one problem or need (SEU, 2005a). Due to the ad hoc definition of age boundaries, the fragmentation of CAMHS and AMHS and the frequent lack or integration of support systems such as housing and education, the transition needs of young people are even less likely to be met (Vostanis, 2005).

Services need to cater for the range of young people's mental health issues, including:

- mental health crisis;
- ongoing mental health problems;
- drug and alcohol misuse;
- early-onset psychotic illness, self-harm and eating disorders;

and attend to the particular needs of:

- young people from minority ethnic communities;
- young people living in rural areas (Smith and Leon, 2001).

Law and policy makers are beginning to acknowledge the importance of providing support for a variety of issues for young people in transition from child and adolescent to adult mental health services. Section 26 of the 2003 Mental Health (Care and Treatment) (Scotland) Act placed new duties on local authorities to provide 'services which are designed to promote the wellbeing and social development' of people who have a mental health disorder, including recreational activities, training and employment assistance (Scottish Executive, 2005, p 13). One solution would be to adopt a holistic approach, which sees the young adult as an individual with a range of issues first, rather than simply focusing on one problem. The advantage of holistic services is that staff could deal with a number of these issues at once in the same location.

Co-located holistic services can make information sharing and onward referral much easier, and mean that young people know where to go for help (Social Exclusion Unit, 2005b). Providing mental health services from nondescript buildings or community centres and attaching them to multidisciplinary teams providing 'one-stop-shop' services could also help to reduce stigma among young adults (Richards and Vostanis, 2004). It has also been argued that a service open to any young adult avoids the stigma that can be attached to targeted services. There would be greater potential for early intervention and support if young adults see services as something for them, rather than feeling they have to fit into a narrowly defined category of need (Howarth and Street, 2000). This would mirror the familiar approach of Connexions, and therefore bridge the gap between services for teenagers and services for young adults.

The way in which advice is presented to these young adults is important in developing trust, which can help in dealing with more complex issues. Homeless young people, for example, are almost three times more likely to experience mental health problems compared to those in stable housing, and one in three will attempt suicide (Howarth and Street, 2000). For these young people, tackling mental health issues is not enough. They would benefit more from receiving support in finding secure housing and employment as well as mental health services. Transition is not just about moving into AMHS – many young people eligible for CAMHS simply do not qualify due to the higher threshold of adult services. The transition out of CAMHS into independent living can be made easier through the use of holistic services to teach these young people key life skills.

Conclusion

It is clear that much can be done to improve the transition of young people with mental health needs from child to adult services. The discrepancies between when CAMHS support ends and AMHS begins in certain parts of the UK mean that young people are not adequately supported. This is exacerbated by the fact that many young people who had been receiving support from CAMHS simply do not qualify for AMHS. Barriers such as the stigma associated with services that have the term 'mental' in their title also have a negative effect on engagement with transitional services among this age group.

By listening to young people who have gone through the process of transition, professionals can ensure that services are developed that will be useful and relevant. Joint working between young people and practitioners working in both child and adult mental health teams can ensure that service users know what to expect when they move into adult services, and have begun to forge relationships before they move. Holistic services, co-located with other services, are accessible and practical for meeting young people's needs in relation not just to mental health, but also issues such as housing and employment. Joint working across the statutory and voluntary sectors, and with the young people who have experienced them, can aid service providers in improving support for young adults in the transitional process from child to adult mental health services.

Key practice points

- Agencies should conduct an audit of their child and adolescent and adult mental health services to ensure that there is no gap in service provision for young people aged between 16 and 18.
- Practitioners working with young adults with mental health needs should develop effective links with wider services, such as housing, employment and care leavers so that they can provide tailored support for individual young people.
- Authorities should ensure that joint training is available for staff in both adults' and children's mental health services to explore issues of collaboration and communication, and support staff implementing this learning in practice through supervision.
- Agencies should consult young people and their families, not only in terms of their own care plans as they move into adult services, but also in the wider design and development of mental health service transition as a whole.
- Practitioners need to acknowledge what is already stable in the young person's life, such as family and friends, and help them to provide additional support for the young person during transition.

> • Local service providers need to ensure that young people living in rural areas can access mental health services easily, and that there is practical provision to enable them to access adult mental health services after transition.

References

Abrams, L., Shannon, S. and Sangalang, C. (2008) 'Transition services for incarcerated youth: a mixed methods evaluation study', *Children and Youth Services Review*, vol 30, no 5, pp 522-35.

Aubrey, C. and Dahl, S. (2006) 'Children's voices: the views of vulnerable children on their service providers and the relevance of services they receive', *British Journal of Social Work*, vol 36, no 1, pp 21-39.

Bamford Review of Mental Health and Learning Disability (NI) (2007) *Bamford review of mental health and learning disability*, Belfast: The Stationery Office.

Buston, K. (2002) 'Adolescents with mental health problems: what do they say about health services', *Journal of Adolescence*, vol 25, no 2, pp 231-42.

Carswell, K., Maughan, B., Davis, H., Davenport, F. and Goddard, N. (2004) 'The psychosocial needs of young offenders and adolescents from an inner city area', *Journal of Adolescence*, vol 27, no 4, pp 415-28.

CSIP (Care Services Improvement Partnership) (2007) Briefing note: Children's services transitions, London: Integrated Care Network.

DCSF (Department for Children, Schools and Families) (2007) *The children's plan: Building brighter futures*, London: DCSF.

DH (Department of Health) (2007) *National Service Framework for Children, Young People and Maternity Services: Core ctandards*, London: DH.

DH (2008) *Transition: Moving on well*, London: DH.

Forbes, A., While, A., Ullman, R., Lewis, S., Mathes, L. and Griffiths, P. (2001) *A multi-method review to identify components of practice which may promote continuity in the transition from child to adult care for young people with chronic illness or disability*, London: National Co-ordinating Centre for NHS Service Delivery and Organisation.

Health and Social Care Advisory Service (2006) *CAMHS to adult transition: HASCAS tools for transition: A literature review for informed practice*, London: Health and Social Care Advisory Service.

Howarth, C. and Street, C. (2000) *Sidelined:Young adults' access to services*, London: New Policy Institute.

Johnson, K. (2003) '"Neighbourhood Watch": transition from child to adult mental health service', *Young Minds Magazine*, no 65, July/August, pp 26-7.

Kurtz, Z., Thornes, R. and Bailey, S. (1998) 'Children in the criminal justice and secure care systems: how their mental health needs are met', *Journal of Adolescence*, vol 21, pp 543-53.

McAuley, C. and Young, C. (2006) 'The mental health of looked after children: challenges for CAMHS provision', *Journal of Social Work Practice*, vol 20, no 1, pp 91-103.

Mental Health Act Commission (2004) *Safeguarding children and adolescents detained under the Mental Health Act 1983 on adult psychiatric wards: Report on the notification and visiting programme by the Mental Health Act Commission between April 2002 and September 2003*, London: The Stationery Office.

NAW (National Assembly for Wales) (2001) *Child and Adolescent Mental Health Services: Everybody's business*, Cardiff: NAW.

Office of the Children's Commissioner (2007) *Pushed into the shadows: Young people's experience of adult mental health facilities*, London: Office of the Children's Commissioner.

OFMDFM (Office of the First Minister and Deputy First Minister) (2006) *Our children and young people – Our pledge*, Belfast: OFMDFM.

Pithouse, A. (2002) 'A National Strategy for Child and Adolescent Mental Health Services in Wales: new challenges and new thinking?', *Research, Policy and Planning*, vol 21, no 1, pp 3-16.

Public Health Institute of Scotland (2003) *Needs assessment report on child and adolescent mental health*, Glasgow: Public Health Institute of Scotland.

Revolving Doors Agency (2002) *Future imperfect?: Young people, mental health and the criminal justice system*, London: Revolving Doors Agency.

Richards, M. and Vostanis, P. (2004) 'Interprofessional perspectives on transitional mental health services for young people aged 16-19 years', *Journal of Interprofessional Care*, vol 18, no 2, pp 115-28.

Ryan, M. (2006) *Transition of adolescents to Adult Mental Health Services*, Totnes: research in practice.

Scottish Executive (2005) *The mental health of children and young people: A framework for promotion, prevention and care*, Edinburgh: Scottish Executive.

SEU (Social Exclusion Unit) (2005a) *Transitions: A Social Exclusion Unit interim report on young adults*, London: Office of the Deputy Prime Minister.

SEU (2005b) *Transitions: Young adults with complex needs: A Social Exclusion Unit final report*, London: Office of the Deputy Prime Minister.

Singleton, N. and Lewis, G. (eds) *Better or worse: A longitudinal study of the mental health of adults living in private households in Great Britain*, London: The Stationery Office.

Smith, K. and Leon, L. (2001) *Turned upside down: Developing community-based crisis services for 16-25-year-olds experiencing a mental health crisis*, London: Mental Health Foundation.

Svanberg, J. and Street, C. (2003) 'Listening to young people: how far inpatient services have still to go to meet young people's needs', *Mental Health Today*, July/August, pp 28-30.

Vostanis, P. (2005) 'Patients as parents and young people approaching adulthood: how should we manage the interface between mental health services for young people and adults?', *Current Opinion in Psychiatry*, vol 18, pp 449-54.

SIX

Transitions for young people seeking asylum

Ravi K.S. Kohli and Helen Connolly

Introduction

> I am a quantum particle trying to locate myself within a swirl of atoms. How much time and energy I'll have to spend just claiming an ordinary place for myself? And how much more figuring out what the place might be, where on earth I might find a stable spot that feels like it's mine, and from where I can observe the world calmly. (Hoffman, 1989, p 160)

We have chosen to begin this chapter by referring to Eva Hoffman's experiences of migration because these reflect, in important respects, some of the core experiences of transitions for people moving from one country to another, from one home to another, and in the case of those seeking asylum, from a place of harm to a place of safety. In all, moving on and settling down are two sides of the same experience of journeys being endured in the hope for stability and the re-emergence of calm. When young people become refugees, they often undertake such extensive journeys towards political, legal and psychological safety. They take risks. They find agents who transport them at a price outward and onward, sometimes to places they do not know, and to people who are strangers. Sometimes they come with siblings, but often they are alone, guarding themselves as they transit across countries and landscapes. They take time to make sense of what has happened to them and with whom and where they belong. In moving, they change in many ways, and as a consequence, while the first stop is safety, their journey has lifelong consequences for them and those around them. In this respect, Turton's (2004) examination of how people make sense of their place and position in a world of movement accurately summarises the transformative nature of forced migration. As forced migrants, these young people make the journey and the journey makes them. Their space and environment, their sense of transplantation and their view of their own identity all shift as the world around them changes.

For those providing care and protection after the border crossing, they are familiar and unfamiliar. They, like any young person growing up, are moving from childhood to adulthood, from dependence to independence, and in some instances from place to place, in seeking opportunities to realise their talents and ambitions, and to take charge of their lives. They are also familiar to those working with vulnerable young people, as a group who face great uncertainty as they move from contexts of danger, to contexts of relative calm. Some of their movements are voluntary. At other times they are pushed and persuaded to move on, sometimes with great force by powerful institutions, mechanisms or factions, and at times such as these, their choices are truncated, and their horizons become hedged with worry. As forced migrants, unlike citizen young people making transitions, their liminality shows itself in different ways. They do not have a country. They are un-located. They wait for long periods for a decision to be allowed to remain. They can be dispersed across the country if powerful agents choose this on their behalf. If they are trafficked, then hidden networks can track them, claim them, and make them disappear from official view. Equally, some can disappear in their own right after having failed in their asylum claims, in trying to remain in the country of asylum.

For all young asylum seekers, the movements range from securely achieving a home and sense of place after obtaining leave to remain in the country, to prolonged, chronic uncertainty about where to go to be safe. In that respect, forced migration yields many trajectories, only some of which are understood by researchers. In these circumstances, assistance that helps them to deal with change and transition can take many forms. In this chapter, we will evaluate the research evidence of the sorts of changes and transitions young people seeking asylum make, and what helps them to feel safe in volatile situations and conditions.

Unaccompanied asylum-seeking young people

An unaccompanied asylum-seeking child is someone who is, or appears to be, under the age of 18, is making an asylum claim on their own behalf, has no adult carer, and needs the care and protection of welfare services in the country of asylum while that claim is examined and settled (UNHCR, 1994). The annual application rate for asylum by children to the UK was about 3,000 per year in 2005 and 2006. Warren (2007) notes that more than 15,000 unaccompanied asylum-seeking children have entered the UK since 2000 and the British Home Office spends more than £140 million per annum primarily through funding councils directly to provide accommodation, care and support services for those children who 'present' in their authority area. There are currently more than 130 local authorities supporting unaccompanied asylum-seeking children but numbers vary widely, with the majority located in London or the South East. In 2007, there were 3,300 unaccompanied minors looked after in England out of a total of 60,000 children and young people (DCSF, 2007). The figures for Scotland and Wales are unclear as they are not maintained by the Scottish Parliament or the Welsh Assembly Government. However, some reports estimate that there were between 100 and 200 unaccompanied children in Scotland in 2006 (Hopkins and Hill, 2006) and about 150 in Wales in 2006 (Warren, 2007).

According to the UK Border Agency's own figures, very few unaccompanied children achieve permanence in the UK at present – about 6-10 out of 100 of their applications for asylum are granted indefinite leave to remain. The majority are given temporary admission until they are close to adulthood, at which point their status is determined in the same way as other adult asylum seekers. In effect, for most unaccompanied minors, future outcomes remain uncertain, and they can live in limbo for substantial periods of their lives after arriving in the UK. What happens to them after they turn 18 is unclear. What is relatively clear is that having begun a journey, they are in charge of their trajectories in very limited ways once it has begun, and it is a process of stop, start and being in limbo – in effect the traffic lights of their lives – that we turn to now.

Forced migration, change and transitions

In understanding forced migration, a simple proposition can be used in relation to the change and transition. *Change* is what happens to you – you become an asylum seeker or refugee because you have to, as the choices that you make are constrained as you flee from disaster. *Transitions* are ways in which you make sense of what has happened to you. Change is therefore external, situational, event based and defined by outcome. It can happen quickly. Transitions, in contrast, are internal, psychological, based on experience, defined in terms of processes and always take time (Bridges, 2004). Bearing these distinctions in mind and the ways in which they connect facts to feelings, can allow those working with unaccompanied asylum-seeking children and young people to frame the depth and dimension of the visible and hidden world they bring as they seek assistance. A relatively robust body of research confirms that when children become refugees or face forced migration for some reason, they differ from each other in the ways that they respond to the pushes, pulls and fluctuating patterns of precarious existence that surround them (Loughry and Eyber, 2003). Some endure, relatively unscathed, and make their ways back to ordinary life over time. A few surrender psychologically when faced with the demolition of the people, places and civic structures that have helped them to grow up. While many recover and go on to lead coherent lives, in some instances, children never regain the elasticity of easy living as they merge into adulthood (McCallin, 1996). While chronic and persistent uncertainty is a known feature of many refugee lives, it is also the case that only a small proportion of refugee children and young people require specialist psychiatric or psychotherapeutic help in order to recover from their past experiences (Richman, 1998; Save the Children, 2003). Between those who are robust and those who remain persistently fragmented, the majority of asylum-seeking and refugee minors deal with changes and transitions at different speeds, depending on their personalities, experiences and circumstances (Kohli, 2007).

Whoever they are, and whatever their trajectories into new territories, the re-growth of predictable life can take time during journeys towards seeking sanctuary. Moreover, in an increasingly volatile environment within many Western countries, such journeys are themselves complex, with temporary admission and return to the country of origin, or another country growing ever more likely for the majority of child asylum applicants (Aynsley-Green, 2006). It is within this frame of ebb and flow, where refugee movements are a problem for some and a solution for others, that we consider their past, present and future lives in terms of the changes asylum-seeking children and young people have to manage, and the transitions they seek to make sense of as they go from the landscapes of their homeland, to another home of their own making.

Leaving the homeland

While life for children seeking asylum is continuous, researchers sometimes approach it as if it were episodic, and certain episodes receive more attention than others. There is, for example, a substantial body of research literature on the process of asylum seeking and resettlement (see below), but very little on understanding the ordinary lives that children led before they became refugees. It is as if the past is another country, which is now lost, taking with it the familiar architecture of living that children grew up within. Moreover, research studies tend to have a spot focus, describing the conditions for children in a particular context of asylum at a particular time, and the thread of time that holds their past present and futures together is seldom tracked longitudinally. As Gifford et al (2007, p 3) suggest, 'the strength of longitudinal designs in studies of refugee resettlement is that they allow us to investigate key transitions and changes in people's lives', yet internationally there are very few research projects tracking the lives of refugee children as they change over time in an asylum country.

In these circumstances, a few researchers have asked children to look back to memories of being at home and moving on. For example, Hopkins and Hill (2006), in refreshingly child-centred research, report that children and young people who came to Scotland as unaccompanied minors had good and bad things to say about the homelands left behind. In living in Scotland, and adjusting to the changes they had to make, they recalled a time and place where the food was good, the people familiar, the culture decipherable and the sun warm (for some at least). What they fervently remembered as bad was the gradual erosion or sudden collapse of civic life and welfare services, the hardening and narrowing of lives through poverty and violence, and the emergent sense of danger brought by war or destitution leading to change and transition. Similarly in England and Holland, refugee children told their stories of a homeland they left with poignant detail (Minority Rights Group International, 1998). Pre-war recollections of solidarity within kinship networks and friends, playtimes, dancing, leavened with the humdrum rhythm of routines, formed a baseline of feeling safe and connected. Yet here again, deprivations in many guises created the pulse of movement outward to foreign countries. Mustafa Mohammed, a Somali young man now living in Holland, recalled the journey out and away from home after the murder of his father in the following way:

> I could not run away because I was so sad about my dead father, and then my mother told me we had to leave Somalia. There were not enough cars and we decided to walk to another city. We walked for two days and a night. Fortunately we had food, but we slept on the ground in the woods until we reached the other city. (Minority Rights Group International, 1998, p 12)

In these circumstances, where life has become increasingly shaped by hostile forces, the routes of exit have to be carefully worked out, if time and resources allow (Ayotte, 2000; Robinson and Segrott, 2002). For children as forced migrants, the sense of belonging defined by the physical and psychological landscape of the homeland is memorised and packed away, to be brought out slowly at a later, safer time and space. In the meantime, as we have noted,

> ... the pegs [of belonging] are uprooted, places abandoned and people and possessions lost in the process of departure from home towards another place, often unknown. Particularly in the shredding of civic obligations during times of civil war, the loss of ordinariness and the absence of rhythm and routine signal the transition from a complex and detailed life to one which is full of risk. Moreover, these events and actions lead to the creation of a compacted identity, where what is most visible is the label on the outside of 'refugee' and 'asylum seeker'. It is by the presentation and judgement of this outside packaging, that the terms of entry into host nations are negotiated.... (Kohli and Mitchell, 2007, p xiii)

Seeking asylum alone

Not all of the passages traversed by lone asylum-seeking children and young people in a host country will be entirely unfamiliar to them. Their itineraries in their new destination may often resonate with the experiences, encounters, rhythms and details of their life, good and bad, from their homeland. The research literature shows that, in seeking to integrate their past and present lives, young asylum seekers are often accomplished in taking charge of the patterns of daily living. These may include experiences of forming and maintaining social networks, doing their best in school and college, engaging in part-time employment and other extra-curricular activities, participating in religious communities and by doing so weaving themselves, as much as the host society permits, into the everyday fabric of their new communities. However, a central and enduring feature of their itinerary – immigration control – with its attendant systems and processes, is unfamiliar. This, more often than not, propels young asylum seekers onto an unaccustomed and arduous voyage. With practically no formal routes accessible for lone children to claim asylum before their arrival in a host country, one of the only means they have of closing the distance between escaping danger and achieving relative security in places such as the UK, is to travel on clandestine journeys that may carry them through to safer contexts. During their transit, young people's thoughts of the physical dangers intrinsic to their journey, their memories of a turbulent homeland and idealised European reception and protection arrangements all coalesce to form hopes of obtaining safety, belonging, success in ways that transform their lives, moving from the edge of a territory to its centre, and from the bottom rung of achievement to the top. However, as noted by one young respondent in the research project described below, the course of their asylum journey moves many from such optimistic imaginations to what the 14th-century Persian poet Mowlana Jalaluddin Rumi described as 'shoreless spaces' (see Arbery, 2005), where horizons are obscured, even though the journey continues.

While it would be wrong of us to suggest that the asylum process is lived and experienced in this way by all unaccompanied asylum-seeking children in the UK, both statistical and qualitative sources substantiate this representation. Current asylum figures demonstrate that the majority of unaccompanied asylum-seeking children are granted, on the grounds of either European human rights law or the unaccompanied asylum-seeking children age concession, what is known as Discretionary Leave to Remain temporarily in the UK. For most young asylum seekers, this status lasts up to their 18th birthday, after which there is no guarantee that their leave will be prolonged. The negative consequences of this system on young asylum seekers' sense of self and belonging has been addressed within the research and advocacy based literature. A pattern of findings suggests that young people live with a sense of a foreshortened future and that there are many adverse implications that this state of mind has on both their emotional health and social integration (Fazel and Stein, 2002; Children's Society, 2006).

The findings of a research project run by one of us (HC) in part echo these views. This research has been exploring with young unaccompanied asylum seekers between the ages of 12 and 21 years, how they feel their asylum and settlement experiences in the UK compare with the rights established in the United Nations Convention on the Rights of the Child. Since the asylum process is central to their itinerary in the UK, it is of no surprise that young people have often reflected upon the asylum process as a stressor that creates both inertia and movement in their worlds. The theme of inertia primarily relates to the lack of status resolution. Only three young people out of the current sample of 18 have had status resolution. The remaining participants have been granted discretionary leave, are still waiting for news after an application to remain or are awaiting deportation to a third country. Young people have expressed how the bureaucratic inertia within the Home Office simultaneously halts their passage to a safe, stable, assimilated and fulfilling life. As such, many have also spoken about their lives lived in the spaces between hope and nowhere.

> "You can't even put your eyes with someone's eyes because we are nothing compared to other people."

> "How hard is that for that person every single day, every single morning, you get up and thinking you are nowhere, from nowhere."

> "It's like giving someone hope and then at the same time taking it away from them."

Resettlement

In the refugee literature, the term 'resettlement' is used in two different ways. The first is formal and refers to the structured migration programmes that are agreed by governments. These permit the movement and permanent remain of a defined quota of refugees from their country of first asylum to a third country (Wright et al, 2004). The second meaning is widely utilised in the psychological and social care literature and refers to the ways in which refugees and asylum seekers reassemble and make sense of their lives within their new environment over time (Kohli, 2007). Adaptation is at the very core of the events and experiences of resettlement and on arrival, unaccompanied asylum seekers have to carry themselves through a number of cultural, social, relational, emotional and practical adjustments. These often include:

- acquiring a new language;
- entering education;
- establishing new friendships and alliances;
- moving into and making a home that is safe and comforting;
- discovering new habits and customs;
- retrieving and maintaining old behaviours and customs;
- developing routines that help to restore ordinary living.

The fundamental difference between the two contexts of resettlement is that the former offers permanence and stability and the second, against the backcloth of restrictive immigration policies, transience and considerable levels of uncertainty. Here, reality becomes one of resettling psychosocially in unsettled circumstances (Wade et al, 2005).

Indeed, one of the fundamental adjustments to be made within the context of forced migration and resettlement is the realisation that life is often not a single voyage but one that is circular, unsustainable and characterised by repeated events of displacement. As such, it is one where many of the changes and transitions that are made within the receiving country may have to be repeated not only on a return to the country of origin but also perhaps even beyond that.

Whatever their future trajectories in terms of resettlement, unaccompanied asylum seekers require care at the point of arrival. This protection mandate is embodied within both domestic and international legislation, primarily in the 1989 Children Act and the 1989 United Nations Convention on the Rights of the Child (Kohli and Connolly, 2008). As part of this duty of care, social work services are obliged, in the same way as they are with citizen children, to offer both practical and pastoral support in relation to establishing stable and safe accommodation, good emotional and physical health, education and training, as well as promoting the cultural, religious and familial identity of young asylum seekers. By respecting all of these duties, social workers act as essential intermediaries in the successful psychosocial resettlement of unaccompanied asylum-seeking children. These duties should almost always be discharged under Section 20 of the 1989 Children Act. This arrangement is necessary if young people are then to qualify for through-care support at the age of 18. Nevertheless, there is empirical evidence, both from our own research, as well as within the wider literature, to suggest that young asylum seekers do not always obtain support under Section 20 but rather under Section 17 of the Children Act (11 Million, 2008). In these circumstances, after-care obligations can be evaded by social work services and as such, young asylum seekers are left to moderate for themselves the risky transitions that arise when they reach the age of 18.

The child welfare literature identifies that the biggest barrier to the successful adaptation of young asylum seekers during the resettlement phase is their unsettled immigration status (Kohli, 2007; Children's Society, 2006). The voices of young people in our research reiterate this issue. For most of the young people who have taken part in the project led by HC, psychological stillness and psychological movement are states that are derived from experiencing life within an ambiguous space. At the core of young people's testimonies of the asylum system is the notion that they want time to stand still, and simultaneously they want it to move on. For some, the longer time flows before a decision is made is experienced as a consolation, a welcome reprieve from past sorrows and a time to live in relative stillness before having to face the very real possibility of another journey, the return journey. The psychological stillness that some young people have spoken of is not only created by the relative safety they have found in the UK but is also enhanced by the various points of anchorage that have been created throughout the duration of their stay. These anchors include accommodation, school and college, friends, kin and professional companions, and we discuss these in the next section of this chapter. The following quotes represent this need for psychological stillness:

> "I got the letter from my solicitor and I was so scared to open it I wish they lose my case and I can never hear about anything like that again. I wish they never contact me again, I am very happy to live like this, not knowing nothing but I am happy the way I am living now and if I don't get a visa or something I am so scared about all this. I don't want them to contact me."

> "I tried to get on with my life not thinking about what was going to happen to me after my 18th birthday because that was when I had to go back to the Home Office and find out what was next."

It is worth considering what internal processes are captured when young people deny, in words, if not in thought, the progress of time and, by implication, their future beyond the final Home Office decision. In the context where young people's itineraries and identities are so profoundly shaped by territorialism, they could be said to be drawing their own borders, ones that divide their internal world from the external world. The deliberate and utopian construction of a personal world that is free from any more moments of departure is therefore, for some, an attempt to prevent the uncertainty of the asylum-seeking process from transgressing their personal borders. It is a defensive, relieving escape from the disquiet and harm that is posed by repatriation and can be interpreted as young people actively searching for the calm that can be found in the structure and regularity of the present. As a coping strategy, their appreciation of the stillness has a similar logic to the process that Papadopoulos (2002) refers to as *psychological hypothermia*, a space that many refugees use to create a sanctuary away from the whirligig of resettlement activities to reflect, to restore and to prepare for letting themselves live again. Papadopoulos (2002) suggests that the central loss for refugees is the loss of home, both as a place and as a way of being. Some of the young people from our research have also positioned the loss and reconstruction of home at the heart of their discussions around psychological stillness. As we have written above, young people associate the movement of time with the finality of status resolution; while resisting time is fundamentally about eclipsing the fear of what lies ahead, whether it is further exposure to danger in the homeland on return, or more simply the fear of blowing about like tumbleweed between countries, and facing one set of rejections after another.

Yet refugee children and young people sometimes show a capacity to root, even in contexts that might move them on. Many appear adept at utilising the transitional space of exile to recreate a sense of belonging and 'home'. Denying the future, therefore, is also a way of holding on tightly to the overall composition and discrete elements of the new life that they have successfully created. We use the phrase 'new life' not to be overly sentimental about the nature of young people's stay in the UK, but to represent the picture most young people in our research have produced of their desire to transcend, to begin again, and to do what Bauman (1996) refers to as *dissolving into place*. Their voices below depict this:

> "I do not regret having come here despite of the situation because something good has come out of it and I will never look back and say that I regret it 'cos I have been given a second chance in life since my arrival in the UK."

> "I just feel like I am born in here. I am learning my life."

The integrative talents of young people are clear in the ways that they use opportunities such as education, new language acquisition, new personal and professional relationships, food and a variety of social and personal mores to swallow and keep down the anxiety of un-belonging. Some evoke memories of their homeland, by joining the rhythms and patterns of past lives with new ones, and others address the chance to start again, and grasp fresh new opportunities for safety, belonging and success.

Food

> "I met an Afghani man at college. I helped him learn computer and when I had a party he said okay you helped me and what do you want me to bring for you. I said my

country food, ask your wife to cook something for me. That was lovely."

"My foster mum, when she does something like make curries I just say my mum's curries taste just like this sort of thing. My mum is always with me."

Personal relationships

"I want to live with who I belong from. Eat Halal food, to know the Koran and if I go to live with a non-Muslim I might be changed and I don't want to be change. You need to be who you are, who you belong."

"I moved to my cousins. That was my decision and I wanted to be with my own family. I really feel happier. I miss my own place, my own language."

Familiar social mores

"Britain is a multiculture and you can see anything in here. You can find your own traditional food from a market or somewhere, you can find your traditional uniform, clothes."

"I asked that I get permanently placed with my second foster carer and so social services decided that this was the best place for me. This has enabled and helped me to practice my own culture, language and religion. She was from the same background as I was and this enabled me to keep up with my religion and it also helped me get to talk and practice more in my own dialect."

Language

"I arrived in the UK in December 2004. I have no English at all and the social worker asked me to go to the college but unfortunately there were no spaces and I realised that all the colleges in the UK start September so they tried to enrol me in different places but I have to wait a long time and finally I got a place in Learn Direct and really I enjoyed learning English."

Service use

"My social worker, I talk to him about everything. My country, my past, what happened. He is calling me, asking me, when he came from holiday he gave me something, a gift and for example, he was leaving me at the age of 16 and he didn't leave me. Do you know when you have to go at 16 and the social worker is going to leave you well I am the only one I think with that social worker that is older than 16…. He is happy for me and I am happy for him."

New friendships

"My foster carer had a three-bedroom house and all I had to do was to share with my other foster sister. We became like real sisters, really close and everyone now thinks we are actually sisters."

"I used to be getting bullied by most of who are my own friends now. They are all friends with me now. They used to, they bullied me 'cos I was looking a different person and now they really help me. They are really coming in my house, they have me in to tea, their parents invite me for dinners and lunch. I just learn from them. My mates teach me, in a good and friendly way and I love it. I just learn more."

Education

"Also it was nice and I started going to college and when I was 13 I stopped going to school in my country because girls are allowed to go to school only up to the age of 13."

New social mores

"When you come with absolutely different clothes and you are kind of shy when you see other people wearing different kinds of things. I didn't come out of my foster carer's house for one week. When she gave me £20 allowance I start buying some t-shirts and some stuff. The clothes is important. I start feeling happy. Some of my dreams I could see coming true, like wearing European clothes."

Additionally, young people have underscored the need for continued support by a number of agencies throughout the difficult transition of childhood to adulthood. This transition is inherently challenging for any young person, in terms of developing their autonomy, negotiating a new social identity, entering further education, training and employment and preparing for independent living. While many young people stress that they would like social services to be a reliable feature in their life, both at the threshold of adulthood and beyond, a number of studies note that this can happen in a piecemeal and unpredictable way (Stanley, 2001; Broad and Robbins, 2005; Wade et al, 2005; Hodes et al, 2008). In our study, young people who have left care have at times spoken of being cut adrift rather than having continued support:

> "At the moment for me, like even I am like a dog. When you separate from social service you miss every help. They don't call me. They don't want to talk to me anymore if I want. Social services should carry on even after 18 for people, for immigrant people, who do not know anything about the system until they are sure that these people can carry on their own and not say goodbye...."

But saying goodbye becomes a reality as young people travelling through the asylum system reach the tipping point of adulthood and the possibilities of detention and removal become real. In these circumstances, transitions can be anticipated through 'triple planning' (Free, 2006). Here, the recommendation is for workers to think and act in unison with the young people to consider one of three possible outcomes:

- first, for the minority, the possibility of resettlement in the UK;
- second, what moving on means for most of them as they reach 'end-of-line circumstances' and prepare for a return to their country of origin or other relevant countries;
- third, doing everything possible to support them while they endure removal and return, including ensuring that they are practically and emotionally ready for departure, and that the circumstances they return to are safe and sustainable.

Returns

Historically in the UK, as in other industrialised nations, the deportation of unaccompanied asylum-seeking children has been comparatively low thus far (Bhabha and Finch, 2006; Free, 2006). Returns before their 18th birthday happen rarely unless there is evidence to suggest that there are adequate reception and support arrangements in their country of origin. Very little is known through research about what creates and sustains successful returns for children. However, what is established is that young people often arrive at the country of asylum as carriers of both family and community hope (Kohli, 2007). In this respect, their lives in their new country are often characterised by a remarkable pressure to accomplish more than just the prize of citizenship. Forced return therefore has the potential to arouse feelings of failure and shame that are equal to or exceed the weight of pre-departure expectation (Rousseau et al, 1998).

Anticipating such circumstances, the Separated Children in Europe Programme has issued guidance that establishes standards of best practice when working with unaccompanied asylum-seeking children, including standards relating to returns. While the emphasis is on safety, there is also guidance on the long-term protection, achievements and reintegration of young people that includes facilitating access to education, vocational training and employment. In one of the only studies to examine the reintegration and psychological health of repatriated and former unaccompanied asylum seekers, Loughry and Flouri (2001) observed that financial security, stable work and education were all considered important to young people on their return to Vietnam. It was also noted within this study that the behavioural adjustment of young people following their return was not problematic and, indeed, they reported fewer difficulties of post-return adjustment than a comparison group of young people who had not been unaccompanied asylum seekers. However, no generalisations can be drawn from one study alone. There is a continued need for research with young people who are returned to different geopolitical contexts. This is particularly pressing in light of UK policies supporting the enforced return of unaccompanied asylum-seeking children whose claims have been refused and appeals are exhausted (Home Office, 2008).

Practice responses

Research shows that unaccompanied minors benefit from trustworthy, reliable and companionable people who are kind, honest, realistic and practically helpful, and who make an effort to understand their world (Kohli and Connolly, 2008). These are the people who are best placed to help them make effective transitions.

Understanding history

While unaccompanied minors may be cautious about discussing any troubling or complex past experiences, establishing a dialogue that encourages the child or young person to unpack the well-remembered habits and customs of life before leaving, appears to be an essential aspect of recovery and resettlement. Workers and carers can try and understand the importance of cultural, social and political aspects of their past lives by reference to films, television, music, literature, the political and economic context of the country, religious beliefs and practices. These broad contextual understandings may – through the child or young person's choosing – be woven into stories of significant personal relationships and the ways these have intersected with personal political affiliations or expressions of faith, and of the reasons for leaving and the journey itself (the decision and decision makers, helpers and companions, risks and opportunities, hopes and fears, and so on). We would, however, suggest that these connections are gently sought at a pace and at a time that is tolerable for the young person, without intrusion and with respect.

Re-establishing ordinary life

The return of the rhythm of ordinary life after having lived through extraordinary events is seen as necessary by unaccompanied minors and helps them to cope with uncertainty produced by the asylum system. Workers and carers can therefore help young people to arrange the ensemble of their new life by facilitating their engagement and achievements in school or college, swift enrolment in English language classes, promoting new friendships with peers and adults, fostering talents and interests, providing extra-curricular activities, and helping unaccompanied children to access places of worship and other cultural signposts such as food shops and community organisations.

Asylum

Social workers and carers are not in a position to offer legal advice, but can secure good legal representation for the child, and ensure that the progress of their claim is kept visible and as high on the agenda as the child needs. With the child's permission, it may be supportive to know the story of asylum as related to the Home Office, so that the child does not continually have to repeat it to different people, and is reassured that a witness to their asylum claim is alongside them. A supportive and knowledgeable adult attending Home Office interviews is seen as practically helpful in many circumstances.

Family tracing

At some point in the asylum journey, an unaccompanied minor may express the wish to trace family members. Not all children embrace the possibility of family tracing with enthusiasm, and many are rightly cautious. Wade et al (2005) urge workers to use available resources such as the British Red Cross or International Social Service, but with the child's knowledge and explicit consent. The ways in which contact is kept up with family members once established – through mail, email, using an intermediary, by telephone or through exchanging tape recordings, for example – need to be pre-planned and financially and practically sustainable for all parties. Whatever the approach to family tracing, a measure of the risks and benefits of exposure of other family members through contact needs to be undertaken regularly. Similarly, some account of the child or young person's capacity to bear unfavourable news about family members needs consideration, within the context of a network of care and support that can care for them when bad news hits.

Resettlement and return

Good practice with unaccompanied asylum-seeking children anticipates the need for a sustainable future, in resettlement or return. Save the Children provides precise information and guidance on how best to plan and involve young people for both of these eventualities (Free, 2006). Indefinite leave to remain in the UK frees young people to move between borders. For those young people whose parents and family are alive, they may wish to travel and be reunited with other family members. In terms of return, plans need to be shaped on an individual basis, taking the context of return into account. Where a young person returns voluntarily, and has used opportunities to develop skills in some practical way, received adequate financial support for return, is able to be safe on return and link up to a network of care and support, the chances of integration are raised. In contrast, an ill-planned forced return after a failed asylum claim to a turbulent context may continue to raise the risks that the young person had sought sanctuary from in the first place.

Key practice points

- Individuals able to offer practical and supportive help to unaccompanied minors are key to effective transitions.

- Young people should be encouraged over time to remember the social and cultural aspects of their past lives and to make connections in their current situation that keeps those aspects alive.

- Unaccompanied minors should be supported to establish the routines of daily life as soon as practicable.

- A knowledgeable adult should be available to support the young person through their application for asylum.

- A careful and considered approach needs to be taken towards family tracing.

- Plans need to be developed for the future, allowing for the outcome to be either resettlement or return.

References

11 Million (2008) *The Children's Commissioner's findings and recommendations regarding the care of unaccompanied asylum seeking children in the London Borough of Hillingdon*, London: 11 Million, www.11million.org.uk/resource/skqu5fbl88a4pyspzqhbz3z6.pdf

Arbery, A.J. (2005) Persian poems: An anthology of verse translations (1st edition), Tehran: Yassavoli Publishers.

Aynsley-Green, A. (2006) *Memorandum from the Office of the Children's Commissioner to the Joint Committee on Human Rights on the Treatment of Asylum Seekers*, 29 September, London: Office of the Children's Commissioner.

Ayotte, W. (2000) *Separated children coming to Western Europe: Why they travel and how they arrive*, London: Save the Children.

Bauman, Z. (1996) 'Assimilation into exile: the Jew as a Polish writer', *Poetics Today*, vol 17, no 4, pp 569-97.

Bhabha, J. and Finch, N. (2006) *Seeking asylum alone: Unaccompanied and separated children and refugee protection in the UK*, A report funded by the John D and Catherine T MacArthur Foundation, Cambridge, MA: Harvard University.

Bridges, W. (2004) *Transitions: Making sense of life's changes*, Cambridge, MA: Da Capo Press.

Broad, B. and Robbins, I. (2005) 'The wellbeing of unaccompanied asylum seeking care leavers', *Diversity in Health and Social Care*, vol 2, no 4, pp 271-7.

Children's Society (2006) *Making a new life in Newham: A study investigating the factors that facilitate young refugee settlement in Newham*, London: Children's Society, www.childrenssociety.org.uk/resources/documents/Project/4291_full. pdf

DCSF (Department for Children, Schools and Families) (2007) *Children looked sfter in England (including adoption and care leavers) year ending 31st March 2007*, First Release, 20 September, London: DCSF.

Fazel, M. and Stein, A. (2002) 'The mental health of refugee children', *Archives of Disease in Childhood*, vol 87, pp 366-70.

Free, E. (2006) *Unaccompanied refugees and asylum seekers turning 18: A guide for social workers and other professionals*, London: Save the Children, www.savethechildren.org.uk

Gifford, S.M., Bakopanos, C., Kaplan, I. and Correa-Velez, I. (2007) 'Meaning or measurement? Researching the social contexts of health and settlement among newly-arrived refugee youth in Melbourne', *Australia Journal of Refugee Studies*, vol 20, no 3, pp 414-40.

Hoffmann, E. (1989) *Lost in translation: A life in a new language*, London: Heinemann.

Hodes, M., Jagdev, D., Chandra, N. and Cunniff, A. (2008) 'Risk and resilience for psychological distress amongst unaccompanied asylum seeking adolescents', *Journal of Child Psychology and Psychiatry*, vol 49, no 7, pp 723-32.

Home Office (2008) *Planning better outcomes: The way forward: Improving the care of unaccompanied asylum seeking children*, www.ukba. homeoffice.gov.uk/sitecontent/documents/aboutus/consultations/ closedconsultations/uasc/

Hopkins, P. and Hill, M. (2006) *This is a good place to live and think about the future: The needs and experiences of unaccompanied asylum-seeking children in Scotland*, Glasgow: Centre for the Study of Child and Society/Scottish Refugee Council.

Kohli, R.K.S. (2007) *Social work with unaccompanied asylum seeking children*, Basingstoke: Palgrave Macmillan.

Kohli, R.K.S. and Connolly, H. (2008) *Fostering children and young people seeking asylum*, London: Community Care Inform, www.ccinform. co.uk

Kohli, R.K.S. and Mitchell, F. (2007) *Working with unaccompanied asylum seeking children: Issues for policy and practice*, Basingstoke: Palgrave Macmillan.

Loughry, M. and Eyber, C. (2003) *Psychosocial concepts in humanitarian work with children: A review of the concepts and related literature*, Washington, DC: National Academies Press.

Loughry, M, and Flouri, E. (2001) 'The behavioural and emotional problems of former unaccompanied refugee children 3-4 years after their return to Vietnam', *Child Abuse and Neglect*, vol 25, pp 249-63.

McCallin, M. (ed) (1996) *The psychological well-being of refugee children: Research, practice and policy issues*, Geneva: International Catholic Child Bureau.

Minority Rights Group International (eds) (1998) *Forging new identities: Young refugee and minority students tell their stories*, London: Minority Rights Group International.

Papadopoulos, R.K. (2002) *Therapeutic care for refugees: No place like home*, Tavistock Clinic Series, London: Karnac.

Richman, N. (1998) *In the midst of the whirlwind: A manual for helping refugee children*, London: Save the Children.

Robinson, V. and Segrott, J. (2002) *Understanding the decision making of asylum seekers*, Finding 172, Research, Development and Statistics Directorate, London: Home Office.

Rousseau, C. (1998) 'Between myth and madness: the pre-migration dream of leaving among young Somali refugees', *Culture, Medicine and Psychiatry*, vol 22, no 4, pp 385-411.

Save the Children (2003) *Young refugees: Providing emotional support to young separated refugees in the UK*, London: Save the Children.

Stanley, K. (2001) *Cold comfort: Young separated refugees in England*, London: Save the Children.

Turton, D. (2004) *The meaning of place in a world of movement: Lessons from long-term field research in Southern Ethiopia*, RSC Working Paper 18, Oxford: International Development Centre, University of Oxford.

UNHCR (United Nations High Commissioner for Refugees) (1994) *Refugee children: Guidelines for protection and care*, Geneva: UNHCR.

Wade, J., Mitchell, F. and Baylis, G. (2005) *Unaccompanied asylum seeking children: The response of social work services*, London: British Association for Adoption and Fostering (BAAF).

Warren, E. (2007) *Planning better outcomes and support for unaccompanied asylum seeking children*, Home Office Consultation Paper: WLGA Briefing, Cardiff: Welsh Local Government Assembly.

Wright, G., Peach, E. and Ward, K. (2004). *Navigation guide to key issues: Resettlement programmes and the United Kingdom*, London: The Information Centre about Asylum and Refugees in the United Kingdom.

SEVEN

From service provision to self-directed support

George Julian

Introduction

The current social care system in the UK is undergoing a period of radical transformation. This transformation and the accompanying transition from service provision to a model of self-directed support forms the focus of this chapter. There are many elements in transition throughout this change as the whole system is redesigned, with an overarching shift from service users as dependent, passive recipients of generic services with very little choice or say in the matter to independent, active decision makers with personalised choices and options available to them. This wholesale transition and the changes associated with it are explored.

Overview of policy and introduction to a system in transition

> Direct payments and individual budgets have been major forces for change in adult social care, and there is considerable policy support for building on current progress and extending these concepts further in future. (Glasby and Duffy, 2007, p 5)

Direct Payments were first introduced in the UK in 1997 when local authorities were given a discretionary power to make payments to disabled people. The 1996 Community Care (Direct Payments) Act and its associated legislation was welcomed by the disability movement and considered a reward for a long campaign by the independent living movement and disabled people who were increasingly dissatisfied with the services available to them (Glasby and Littlechild, 2006). In 2003, the power to provide Direct Payments was replaced by a requirement for all local authorities to offer them to those assessed as needing community care services who wished to have them and were capable of managing their own support, with or without assistance (DH, 2003; Scottish Executive, 2003).

Ten years on from their introduction, the 2006 White Paper *Our health, our care, our say* (DH, 2006a) continues to add support to the policy of Direct Payments. The White Paper considers Direct Payments as key to personalised services and also made a commitment to developing a risk framework. The first update on the progress towards the goals in the White Paper – *Making it happen* (DH, 2006b) – includes a road map that plots the actions for implementation. It states that:

> Working with CSIP [Care Services Improvement Partnership], we will gather and disseminate good practice and increase awareness of the benefits of direct payments among local authority frontline workers, senior staff and elected members, as well as among people who need support and their carers. (DH, 2006b, p 16)

The government policy and guidance documents on Direct Payments have been continually amended and altered over the past 10 years in an attempt to widen the eligibility criteria for Direct Payments and increase take-up (2000 Community Care [Direct Payments] Amendment Regulations; 2000 Carers and Disabled Children Act; 2001 Health and Social Care Act; 2002 Carers and Direct Payments Act [Northern Ireland]; DH, 2003, 2004; CSCI, 2004; WAG, 2004; Cabinet Office and DH, 2005; DH and CSIP, 2006). During this time, much has been written offering philosophical and conceptual commentary on Direct Payments and discussing the key issue of take-up (such as most recently Pearson, 2006; Davey et al, 2007; Priestley et al, 2007). It is also worth noting that the number of people taking up Direct Payments in Scotland, while increasing, is still significantly smaller (proportionately half the number of users) than in England (Pearson, 2006).

Individual Budgets have emerged as a key element of more recent government policy and are designed to focus on the joint principles of service user choice and control. While Direct Payments have led to many improvements for those using them, their success has been somewhat limited by the traditional system. They allow people to be creative with how they design their support, but the systems through which they access it have not changed. The process of assessment and the way in which most social care funds are spent has not altered and

Direct Payments have not led to a wide change in culture for service users or those working in adult social care. Individual Budgets, with their focus on choice and control and explicit philosophy of changing the system, are seen to offer all of the benefits of Direct Payments alongside the opportunity of whole-scale transformation (Glasby and Duffy, 2007).

The intention behind Individual Budgets is that individuals who need social care and related services will have a clear idea of the resources at their disposal. This in turn should enable them to make their own choices about how best to use the money allocated to them to design the support that they want. The commitment to piloting an Individual Budget scheme was first made in policy documents published in early 2005. These included *Improving the life chances of disabled people* (Cabinet Office, 2005), *Opportunity age* (DWP, 2005), *Independence, well-being and choice* (DH 2005) and *Our health, our care, our say* (DH, 2006a). The two-year Individual Budget pilot programme was launched in 2006 and involved 13 local authorities across England. The large-scale evaluation made use of a randomised controlled trial that looked at the costs, outcomes and cost-effectiveness of Individual Budgets by comparing the experiences and outcomes for those receiving an Individual Budget with those who accessed conventional methods of service delivery (IBSEN, 2008).

The end of 2007 saw the publication of *Putting people first* (DH, 2007), a cross-government framework for transforming adult social care, centred around four key principles:

- access to universal services;
- prevention and early intervention;
- choice and control;
- social capital.

The focus is on radically improving people's experience of local support and services. There is a clear commitment to completely redesigning the social care system and explicit acknowledgement that the participation of users and carers is key to the success of this. 'It recognises that sustainable and meaningful change depends significantly on our capacity to empower people who use services and to win the hearts and minds of all stakeholders, especially front line staff' (DH, 2007, p 1).

The local authority circular *Transforming social care* (DH, 2008a) stated the framework plans for making the system transformation happen and made a commitment to new resources in the form of the transformation reform grant. A year later, following a recommendation in Lord Darzi's review of the National Health Service (NHS) (DH, 2008c), a pilot of personal health budgets was announced in the 2009 Health Bill. The Bill focuses on additional ways of giving patients greater choice and control, or personalisation, over the health services that they require.

No one can be in any doubt that the adult social care system is currently undergoing a huge transition. Alan Johnson, Secretary of State for Health, at the launch of *Putting people first*, described the transition as:

> ... a major redistribution of power from the State to the Citizen according with the fundamental human right to self-determination. This has the potential to be one of the most radical Public Service reforms for a generation. 21st Century social justice with an active and empowering state, rather than one which is paternalistic and controlling. (Johnson, 2007)

A number of elements of the system that are undergoing change are discussed in the remainder of this chapter.

Developments in Scotland have tended to mirror those south of the border, although the pace of change has been somewhat slower, with the Scottish Executive slow to respond to *Improving the life chances of disabled people* (Cabinet Office, 2005) and reluctant to make commitments to self-directed support (Pearson, 2006). The Scottish Executive issued guidance in July 2007 identifying a number of key interventions that local authorities could implement to increase take-up of self-directed support (Scottish Executive, 2007).

While self-directed support has gained steady momentum in England and Scotland, to date progress has been slower in Wales and Northern Ireland. In Wales there has been some developing activity with the establishment of a partnership between organisations committed to the principles of self-directed support. These organisations (including seven local authorities) now form **in Control Cymru**. The first small-scale pilot of Individuals Budgets in Wales took place in Wrexham. Despite a strong history of person-centred planning in Wales, to date there has been no commitment from the Welsh Assembly Government to move towards a system of self-directed support.

Progress in Northern Ireland has been even slower, with steps just being taken to consider how self-directed support can work. **in Control Northern Ireland** was established in 2008 and it is working with the Southern Health and Social Service Board and the Southern Health and Social Care Trust to develop self-directed support.

Introduction to the evidence base

Over the past decade, there have been a number of studies that have explored the use of Direct Payments and Individual Budgets and other alternative models of social care support. This research has explored the experience from the perspective of those receiving services and those who work in adult social care. There are some limitations to this evidence, such as:

- the predominance of small-scale research;
- the relatively limited timescale within research studies for observing significant system changes;
- the fact that social care provision is constantly transitioning and developing;
- the pilot nature of some of the studies, leading to exceptional enthusiasm for the approach, combined with dedicated supports, which may not translate into wider system changes.

However, exploring the evidence about what is known allows for a number of common issues to be highlighted and these are addressed below.

Cultural change and transition

> The key message for practice ... is that cultural change and service user involvement are inherently linked. Improving the practice around user involvement at all levels – which is cultural change in itself – is the key to improving change in all other aspects of service provision. (SCIE, 2007, p 78)

This key message is taken from a knowledge review commissioned by the Social Care Institute for Excellence. It makes it clear that the most significant transition required for the successful change of provision is one of attitudes and cultural change and the fact that these need to be all encompassing. This shifting mindset, accompanied by the adoption of new roles and ways of working, requires a complete shift not only in professional roles but also in the expectations of service users.

Social care provision in the UK has evolved from large-scale institutional care, to large building-based services commissioned in block contracts such as residential homes or day centres, to a focus on personalised care and community-centred services over the past two decades. Individual people using services, together with service user groups and the independent living movement, have campaigned for the right for individual choice for many years.

One of the organisations that have been very involved in the development of an individualised, person centred approach is **in Control**. It has played a pivotal role in the redesign of the social care system and has been working on developing a new operating system, with a focus on active citizenship, since it was set up in 2003. Established as a social enterprise with a number of partners including the Department of Health, the primary focus of **in Control** was 'to explore ways in which the current system of social care might be reformed, in particular to develop a pragmatic and universal model of Self-Directed Support to progress the personalisation of social care services' (Hatton et al, 2008, p 9).

in Control's initial work was with people with learning disabilities but it now works with all groups of people requiring support, alongside staff in adult social care, children's services and a number of primary care trusts.

Central to the **in Control** philosophy and approach is a required change in the power relationship that exists between those receiving support and the service professionals involved. **in Control** has pioneered a move away from a traditional 'professional gift model' where professionals held power, to a 'citizenship model' that holds the person using services at the very centre of all decisions made. To find out more about the work of **in Control**, visit their website (www.in-control.org.uk), which has a wealth of resources and publications, including further information on the thinking and philosophy of self-directed support

The changing role of service users

> The participative approach turns on its head traditional public service organisation. Traditional approaches put professionals at the centre of the process; participative approaches put the individual in charge.... Self-directed services put the person at the centre of the action. (Leadbeater et al, 2008, p 10)

The original impetus for changing the social care system came from service users. The activism of individuals and small groups of service users who were unhappy with their current support provision and who demanded more flexible support was critical to securing the Direct Payment legislation and accompanying changes (Glasby and Littlechild, 2006; Pearson and Riddell, 2006). *Improving the life chances of disabled people* (Cabinet Office, 2005) not only made a commitment to piloting Individual Budgets but it also framed Direct Payments as a means of facilitating the independent living agenda. The focus on partnership and personalisation, alongside a call for widespread reform, is echoed in more recent policy such as *Putting people first* (DH, 2007) and is at the centre of developing practice.

The traditional approach to social care was based on a professional assessing a person's needs, devising a care plan for them and allocating them services. The role of the service user within this process was at best someone who was consulted, at worse someone who was a passive recipient processed through the system. In contrast, self-directed support holds service users at the core. Its success is entirely dependent on service users being active participants in the process. Service users are provided with more choice and control, they are actively involved in the assessment process, in identifying the outcomes that they hope for, in shaping what support they require and in choosing who provides it for them (Leadbeater, 2004; Glasby and Duffy, 2007).

Leadbeater et al (2008) consider that transformation as a result of self-directed services has five key ingredients:

- *Attitude change of service users towards themselves and the role that they play.* Service users who had traditionally been passive recipients of care now have an active role in planning and commissioning the services that they would like. Evidence gathered during the evaluation of Individual Budgets clearly shows that those individuals who received an Individual Budget were significantly more likely to report feeling in control of their daily lives, compared to those in receipt of traditional services (IBSEN, 2008). Research that looked at service users' experience of self-directed support in Scotland showed similar findings, with the overwhelming experience of service users being a positive one, with a focus on flexibility, control, choice and independence (SGSR, 2008).
- *Change in relationships between service users and professionals.* Traditionally, 'professionals' assessed what service a person required, planned and provided services for them and often they were also responsible for judging the quality of that service and the outcomes on the person's behalf. Self-directed services turn this model on its head; professionals have a role of supporting people to make better choices for themselves, while retaining the critical overview of quality of services; and service users play a far more active role in the assessment of, and provision for, their own needs.

- *New knowledge and information, which shape services.* Traditionally, professionals were expected to assess service users and design services or solutions for passive recipients. The new emphasis on self-directed services allows for knowledge to be collected from previously untapped sources such as service users, their families, friends and community members.
- *Services and providers have to respond to service user demand.* This has meant a move away from large-scale block contracts such as day centres and residential homes to more individualised and personalised services organised around the individual service user's home.
- *Power shift to the service users at the heart.* All of these changes mean that service users are truly at the heart of their provision and they therefore have a responsibility to set goals and identify the outcomes that they wish to achieve. The responsibility for assessing and managing risks and for accounting for how resources are used also shifts to the service user.

Putting people first (DH, 2007) is explicit that success in personalisation is dependent on a real cultural shift to one of shared ownership and direction; the prerequisite for this success is the commitment of all stakeholders – service users, carers and staff. The role of user-led organisations is discussed below.

The role of user-led organisations

Putting people first sets out a key objective:

> Support for at least one local user led organisation and mainstream mechanisms to develop networks which ensure people using services and their families have a collective voice, influencing policy and provision. (DH, 2007, p 4)

User organisations have been heavily involved in the development of the self-directed support agenda to date and the key role that they play is clearly acknowledged in recent research and policy (DH, 2007; IBSEN, 2008; SGSR, 2008).

Scottish research acknowledges the strength of a well-established user movement in providing the basis for developing shared visions and commitments to delivering self-directed support (SGSR, 2008). In England, the Individual Budget evaluation (IBSEN, 2008) found that in a number of authorities, user-led organisations were being considered as hosts or providers of support planning and brokerage services. This option has a number of advantages, for example being seen as independent of social services and having strong existing links with the disability movement with an associated positive image and closer links to service users and carers. *Putting people first* (DH, 2007) recognises the ongoing pivotal role for user-led organisations and puts the onus on local authorities to develop forums, networks and other opportunities for service users, carers and staff to all contribute to the change process.

Essex Coalition of Disabled People (ECDP) was established in 1995 to enhance the lives of disabled people in Essex and beyond. 'We provide a wide range of support, information, advice and guidance services. We also play a key role in influencing the agenda of tomorrow to effect real social change to enhance the everyday lives of disabled people". ECDP provides a range of supports for Direct Payment users and was heavily involved in the Essex Individual Budgets Pilot. To find out more visit, www.edcp.org.uk

Guidance published in support of *Putting people first* (DH, 2009) recommends that local authorities consider the following when engaging with user-led organisations: dialogue, recognition, delivery, (the need to) embed, support and links.

The changing role of social workers

In 2006, the *Options for excellence* report was published in England (DH, 2006c). It brought together two government departments (Health and Education and Skills) and a number of strands of work to explore the future of the social care workforce in England. Similarly, *Changing lives* (Scottish Executive, 2006) in Scotland also looked to the future of the profession and the current Northern Ireland Social Care Council Roles and Tasks of Social Work Project (Bogues, 2008) is exploring this issue. All of the reviews have explored how the workforce would need to adapt for future emerging roles, with an emphasis on flexibility and creativity.

At the start of 2008, the General Social Care Council published a long-awaited statement on the roles and tasks of social workers (GSCC, 2008), locating social work skills within the current transformational context, applying and extending the principles of personalisation. *Putting people first* (DH, 2007) identified a clear vision for the role of social care staff in England: social care staff are to ensure that people achieve their maximum potential and have the opportunity to exercise choice and control over their lives, and to facilitate them to achieve the outcomes that they seek.

The transition to a system of self-directed support seems to present opportunities and challenges in equal measure for social work staff. Some consider that the development of their role from one of a gatekeeper or resource manager, into one with more of a focus on facilitation, brokerage and supporting individuals to make decisions and choices for themselves, is a very positive move. There is much talk about a return to traditional social work values and that the changes present an opportunity for social work to reaffirm its role. On the other hand, there is still a sense of uncertainty about the changing roles and some social workers are concerned that there would be a fragmentation of the care management process and that their professional skills would not be seen as necessary (IBSEN, 2008; SGSR, 2008).

What is clear from the research into Direct Payments and Individual Budgets is that social care staff play a critical role in their success. Where staff are enthusiastic and knowledgeable, uptake is much higher than in situations where staff are unsure or hostile (Hasler, 2003; Spandler and Vick, 2004; Newbigging and Lowe, 2005; Pearson, 2006; SGSR, 2008). One key ingredient for ensuring the support of staff is training; the evaluation of the Individual Budgets pilot found an overwhelming feeling that more and better training was needed to address issues such as assessment, support planning, brokerage, knowledge of services, and practical aspects to holding an Individual Budget such as employing staff, managing finances and managing risk (IBSEN, 2008). Likewise, Scottish research has found that limited training on self-directed support was restricting uptake (SGSR, 2008). When staff feel confident about self-directed support, are knowledgeable about procedures and options available and, most importantly, are convinced of the benefits of changing approach, then success will follow.

When Individual Budgets were first talked about I have to be honest and admit that I immediately adopted the ostrich attitude. I put my head in the sand and pretended it had nothing to do with me. I stayed in this position for several months, through various training and working group sessions, until I finally realised the significance of what Individual Budgets were about and the potential available for the young people and their families with whom I work.

Slowly, very slowly, it dawned on me that there was the opportunity to be a part of something that would change the way that young people in transition are assessed and offered services. It was time to move from the traditional way of working to something that was more person centred, to give young people and their families the chance to have more say about the services that they are offered and how they would like to be supported. (Steve Shaw, community care worker; cited in Coventry University, 2007, p 31)

Support planning and brokerage

> Support is needed for people using SDS [self-directed support]. It is important that this is recognised as some people mistakenly understand SDS to mean that people simply 'get on with it' for themselves. People will need varying degrees of support both in planning how to use their budgets (support planning) and in organising the components needed to deliver their plan (support brokerage). (Henwood and Hudson, 2007, p 5)

Following the publication of *Putting people first* (DH, 2007), the Department of Health issued an interim statement in relation to the adult social care workforce strategy (DH, 2008b). This statement clearly identifies some of the key issues and strategic priorities for the workforce as it seeks to take forward the vision of self-directed support. It states:

> It will mean the workforce assuming a more proactive and enabling role in how they respond to people's needs and preferences but having far less control over the details of the support that people receive – taking on roles which strongly focus on brokerage, information and service advocacy. (DH, 2008b, p 4)

When Individual Budgets were introduced, the intention was that support planning and brokerage would replace traditional care planning, supporting people to decide how their budget could be used to pursue their outcomes, as identified in the initial assessment process. The increased flexibility and choice that result from this approach have produced both benefits and challenges; some staff have welcomed the role and feel that they have more creativity; others have felt that the burden of paperwork is too onerous and that their skills are being lost (IBSEN, 2008). In a context of increasing self-directed support, there is a role for social workers to play more creative and person–centred roles. Leadbeater et al (2008) identify a number of possible roles:

- *advisers* – providing support to individuals to self-assess their needs, identify their desired outcomes and plan their support;
- *navigators* – steering individuals through the system to the support services that they want;
- *brokers* – supporting individuals to pull together the elements of their care package from a number of different sources;
- *service providers* – using traditional social work skills such as therapeutic/counselling skills with individuals;
- *risk assessors and auditors* – providing support, especially in complex cases;
- designers of the social care system – facilitating relationships between all providers, for example the formal, informal, voluntary and private sectors.

Risk and risk management

There can be no doubt that self-directed support brings the issue of risk to the fore. In traditional services, the duty of care, that is the responsibility for ensuring that service users are not at risk of harm, rests with the local authority and service providers; this can often lead to complaints of people being overprotected and creativity being stifled. Self-directed support tips the balance and engages individuals with managing their own risk, leading to a shared ownership of risk and a much greater potential for risk taking (Leadbeater et al, 2008).

Self-directed support is underpinned by a philosophy of positive risk taking; indeed, for some recipients of Individual Budgets, it is reported that this is the principal benefit for them of using this provision (IBSEN, 2008). To date there is no strong evidence that service users are at increased risk as a result of self-directed services; in fact, there is a growing argument that self-directed support leads to decreased levels of risk as people have wider networks of support; support packages that are designed with the help of family and friends with more detailed knowledge than a social worker alone could provide; a sense of shared responsibility and more effective checks within the system to eliminate undue risks (IBSEN, 2008; Leadbetter et al, 2008).

What is clear from the evidence to date is that staff have many concerns about risk and self-directed support. The Individual Budgets evaluation showed that care coordinators had difficulty in changing their culture in light of concerns around safeguarding. Staff concerns centred on the risks of 'poorer quality services, misuse of funds, financial abuse, neglect and harm' (IBSEN, 2008, p 249). Staff were also unsure about how much responsibility for risk sat with the holder of the Individual Budget, how risks should be managed and what the implications were for the safeguarding of vulnerable adults. The concern mentioned most frequently was the lack of Criminal Record Bureau checks on those employed directly by Individual Budget holders. These concerns need to be addressed so that staff fears are allayed and transition towards the new way of working is not disrupted.

Service provision and the market

> Self-directed services will work only as the product of a collaborative innovation involving a variety of players in a community. (Leadbeater et al, 2008, p 63)

It is still relatively early in the transition from traditional services to those provided through self-directed support and therefore there is a not a lot of evidence of what works best. A small number of providers and commissioners of services were interviewed during the evaluation of the Individual Budget pilot and they reported that they welcomed the opportunity that Individual Budgets had presented to expand their services and develop new and innovative ways to support clients (IBSEN, 2008).

As the adult social care system transitions towards services accessed through self-directed support, traditional services will undoubtedly change. There will almost certainly be a reduction in local authority block contracts and large-scale service provision, in favour of more flexible, local, small-scale and personalised provision based in the community. Experience to date suggests that the transition towards personalised services will be a gradual, not revolutionary, change; however, it is certain that 'traditional service providers – public, private and voluntary – will face upheaval and change' (Leadbeater et al, 2008, p 59).

One of the advantages of this changing market is that providers are forced to become more person centred, to offer more flexibility to the service user and to think creatively about the supports that are available. While services offered in-house by local authorities are likely to experience a decrease in demand, there will be other pivotal roles for local authorities to fulfil. One such role is the strategic informing or shaping of the market – service users and providers – of what services are available or required at a local level:

Major challenges will arise as existing contracts with providers come up for renewal, and local authorities will need to work carefully with providers to ensure that new contracts can support new patterns of user demand while at the same time protecting providers from excessive – and ultimately destabilising – risk. Managing local markets to provide individualised services will be a major challenge in the future. (IBSEN, 2008, pp 250-1)

Councils will also be expected to work alongside service users and those providing services to ensure high standards (IBSEN, 2008; Leadbeater et al, 2008).

> shop4support is a collaboration between **in Control** and Valueworks. Established as a social enterprise, it is a website where people can go to look for the support that they want. 'Its core purpose is to build a retail market place for health and social support that creates better value for citizens through offering a choice of focussed services and by helping them to control their support, their money and their lives.' It allows those offering support services to advertise and those looking for support to explore what is available in their local area. For more information, visit www.shop4support.com

One of the frequently raised concerns about self-directed support services is that for some, such as those living in rural areas, the market offers no choice. While having a personalised budget will not necessarily impact on the options available to the budget holder, it does potentially enable the budget holder to think creatively and develop an individual solution that works in their community. Many people used Direct Payments to access more personalised support through employing personal assistants; self-directed support will take this potential a step further and enable service users to utilise their own networks that would not normally be involved in providing services (Manthorpe and Stevens, 2008).

Key ingredients for change

The approach that is needed in personalisation requires a different way of thinking and behaving and this can be an extremely uncomfortable and challenging process. (Henwood and Hudson, 2007, p 3)

Self-directed support is the model of future provision in adult social care and, for it to be successful, a considerable transformation is required. The model and philosophy of support provision are in a state of flux; the transition from traditional service provision to personalised models of support has started. Some local authorities are trailblazing, forging ahead with new approaches to self-directed support, others are slightly more hesitant, and still some are reluctant to make the required moves. This final section explores what we know can help with the change process in the form of leadership and communication.

Leadership

Enthusiasm and commitment to the philosophy and objectives of self-directed support do not in themselves translate into change without leadership and support (Henwood and Hudson, 2007). The clear need for strategic leadership has been shown in evaluations of self-directed support in Scotland and in the Individual Budget pilots (IBSEN, 2008; SGSR, 2008). Leadership needs to come from the very top; political support is seen as critical to helping managers handle the risks that are inevitable in such a transition. One considerable risk is that the move to self-directed support is seen as a money-saving venture; to allay this concern, an alliance of senior managers and politicians who believe in the philosophy and think that it is the right thing to do, not just a cost-cutting exercise, is recommended (Leadbeater et al, 2008). Those people leading the transitional process need to be able not only to articulate the improvements and potential of the new approach, but also to demonstrate that they have considered the potential impact that the change will have on service users, staff, providers and the local community.

Communication

The shift to self-directed support requires a number of significant cultural changes (as identified above) and all the key players need to adjust the part that they play in the system. Therefore an investment in support for communication is essential (IBSEN, 2008; SGSR, 2008). The evaluation of the Individual Budgets pilots showed that communication and awareness-raising events often fell into the remit of training; it is argued that this reflects the need for a significant cultural shift for successful implementation (IBSEN, 2008). Communication refers to the need for staff members to acquire new communication skills to encourage service users to make their own choices, rather than to control services for them. It also refers to public awareness-raising events to raise the profile and status of self-directed support and introduce the system to service users and staff. One of the most successful communication techniques has been to facilitate a service user to come and share their story about what has worked for them. It is hard to argue with success. 'In the instances where it's worked well for people and they're really happy.... That makes me enthusiastic about it' (care coordinator, learning disability team) (IBSEN, 2008, p 44).

A number of authorities have utilised service user experiences through requesting that they speak at events or record their stories on a DVD or in a film. Coventry City Council, one of the 13 authorities involved in piloting Individual Budgets, also commissioned their own independent evaluation from Coventry University to focus on service users' experiences. This evaluation used scrapbooks, short films, blogs and the collective production of a huge jigsaw, to enable service users and their carers to share their experiences in their own way.

Conclusion

The transition from traditional service provision to personalised, self-directed support services is well under way. It is clear that this change will have a widespread impact on many people – service users and staff. It is essential that we consider the many different elements that have come into play as a result of such a huge cultural shift and identify how best we can support service users, staff and providers throughout.

Key practice points

- Actively involve service users and frontline staff in developing new systems right from the beginning – involve them in the very first conversations and ensure that they are involved throughout.
- Leadership from the top – involve your local authority councillors; brief them on the benefits of adopting a self-directed support approach and introduce them to service users who have benefited from the changes.
- Consider establishing a dedicated self-directed support team who are easily contactable, knowledgeable and skilled – they will be essential in supporting service users and staff to cope with the required changes.
- Share success stories – ensure that these include the everyday as well as the exceptional; capture them in a way that harnesses the service user's voice and share them far and wide.
- Face your fear – change can be challenging and it is usual to feel anxious; discuss your concerns with your colleagues and try to keep a solution focus – concentrate on the opportunities that self-directed support provides.
- Learn more – talk to service users, read newsletters, attend briefings, actively participate in training events. The more you learn the more confident you will be in the new system.

References

Bogues, S. (2008) *People Work not just paperwork: What people told us during the consultation conducted for the NISCC Roles and Tasks of Social Work Project*, Belfast: Northern Ireland Social Care Council.

Cabinet Office (2005) *Improving the life chances of disabled people*, London: Cabinet Office.

Cabinet Office and DH (Department of Health) (2005) *Making a difference: Direct Payments*, London: Cabinet Office.

Coventry University (2007) *Individual Budgets in Coventry: Our stories*, Coventry: Coventry City Council.

CSCI (Commission for Social Care Inspection) (2004) *Direct Payments: What are the barriers?*, London: CSCI.

Davey, V., Snell, T., Fernández, J.-L., Knapp, M., Tobin, R., Jolly, D., Perkins, M., Kendall, J., Pearson, C., Vick, N., Swift, P., Mercer, G. and Priestley, M. (2007) *Schemes providing support to people using Direct Payments: A UK survey*, London: Personal Social Services Unit.

DH (Department of Health) (2003) *Direct Payments guidance: Community care, services for carers and children's services (Direct Payments) guidance*, London: The Stationery Office.

DH (2004) *Direct choices: What councils need to make Direct Payments happen for people with learning disabilities*, London: The Stationery Office.

DH (2005) *Independence, well-being and choice: Our vision for the future of social care for adults in England*, London: The Stationery Office.

DH (2006a) *Our health, our care, our say*, London: The Stationery Office.

DH (2006b) *Our health, our care, our say: Making it happen*, London: The Stationery Office.

DH (2006c) *Options for excellence: Building the social care workforce of the future*, London: The Stationery Office.

DH (2007) *Putting people first: A shared vision and commitment to the transformation of adult social care*, London: The Stationery Office.

DH (2008a) *Transforming social care*, Local Authority Circular (DH) (2008) 1, London: DH.

DH (2008b) *Putting people first: Working to make it happen: Adult social care workforce strategy – interim statement*, London: The Stationery Office.

DH (2008c) *High quality care for all: NHS Next Stage review final report*, London: The Stationery Office.

DH (2009) *Putting people first: Working together with user-led organisations*, London: The Stationery Office.

DH and CSIP (Department of Health and Care Services Improvement Partnership) (2006c) *Direct payments for people with mental health problems: A guide to action*, London: The Stationery Office.

DWP (Department for Work and Pensions) (2005) *Opportunity age: Meeting the challenge of ageing in the 21st century*, London: The Stationery Office.

Glasby, J. and Duffy, S. (2007) *Our health, our care, our say: What could the NHS learn from Individual Budgets and Direct Payments?*, Birmingham: Health Services Management Centre/in Control.

Glasby, J. and Littlechild, R. (2006) 'An overview of the implementation and development of direct payments', in J. Leece and J. Bornat (eds) *Developments in Direct Payments*, Bristol: The Policy Press, pp 19-32.

GSCC (General Social Care Council) (2008) *Social work at its best: A statement of social work roles and tasks for the 21st century*, London: GSCC.

Hasler, F. (2003) *Clarifying the evidence on Direct Payments into practice*, London: National Centre for Independent Living.

Hatton, C., Waters, J., Duffy, S., Senker, J., Crosby, N., Poll, C., Tyson, A., O'Brien, J. and Towell, D. (2008) *A report on in Control's second phase: Evaluation and learning 2005-2007*, London: in Control Publications.

Henwood, M. and Hudson, B. (2007) *Evaluation of the Self-Directed Support Network: An overview of key messages*, London: Department of Health.

IBSEN (Individual Budgets Evaluation Network) (2008) *Evaluation of the Individual Budgets pilot programme: Final report*, York: Social Policy Research Unit.

Johnson, A. (2007) 'Putting people first', Speech, 10 December, www.dh.gov.uk/en/news/speeches/DH_100286

Leadbeater, C. (2004) *Personalisation through participation: A new script for public services*, London: DEMOS.

Leadbeater, C., Bartlett, J. and Gallagher, N. (2008) *Making it personal*, London: DEMOS.

Manthorpe, J. and Stevens, M. (2008) *The personalisation of adult social care in rural areas*, Gloucester: Commission for Rural Communities.

Newbigging, K. and Lowe, J. (2005) *Direct Payments and mental health: New directions*, Brighton: Pavilion Publishing.

Pearson, C. (ed) (2006) *Direct Payments and personalisation of care*, Edinburgh: Dunedin Academic Press.

Pearson, C. and Riddell, S. (2006) 'Introduction: the development of direct payments in Scotland', in C. Pearson (ed) *Direct Payments and personalisation of care*, Edinburgh: Dunedin Academic Press, pp 1-12.

Priestley, M., Jolly, D., Pearson, C., Riddell, S., Barnes, C. and Mercer, G. (2007) 'Direct Payments and disabled people in the UK: supply, demand and devolution', *British Journal of Social Work*, vol 37, no 7, pp 1189-204.

SCIE (Social Care Institute for Excellence) (2007) *Developing social care: Service users driving culture change*, London: SCIE.

Scottish Executive (2003) *Social Work (Scotland) Act 1968: Sections 12B and C – Direct Payments: Policy and practice guidance*, Edinburgh: Scottish Executive.

Scottish Executive (2006) *Changing lives: Report of the 21st century social work review*, Edinburgh: Scottish Executive.

Scottish Executive (2007) *National guidance on self-directed support*, Edinburgh: Scottish Executive.

SGSR (Scottish Government Social Research) (2008) *A review of self-directed support in Scotland*, Edinburgh: Crown Copyright, www.scotland.gov.uk/Publications/2008/05/30134050/0

Spandler, H. and Vick, N. (2004) *Direct Payments, independent living and mental health*, London: Health and Social Care Advisory Service.

WAG (Welsh Assembly Government) (2004) *Direct Payments guidance: Community care, services for carers and children's services (direct payments) guidance*, Cardiff: WAG.

EIGHT

Transitions to supported living for older people

Alison Petch

Introduction

> Decisions about care-home placement are complex and
> involve many stakeholders, multiple decisions, distinct
> phases, several modes of interaction between the actors, and
> variable outcomes that are provisional and may change over
> time. (Davies and Nolan, 2003, p 444)

The title for this chapter has been carefully selected. Older people who
require support on the grounds of disability or increasing age are likely
to experience a range of transitions. At one end of the continuum may
be the shift from independence to the acknowledgement of the need
for a modest degree of support in maintaining daily life; at the other
may be the move to 24-hour support within a care home. At various
points in between, individuals may move to live with family, may toy
with alternative models such as co-location or may access various
forms of telecare support. This chapter explores both the transition
from independence to a degree of dependence on support from others
within the same place, reflecting the current focus on ageing in place,
and the transition through a physical move, for example to extra-care
housing or a care home. The discussion will relate to the core elements
of independence, well-being and choice at the heart of the adult social
support agenda. It will include an exploration of the impact on family
members at key points of transition, and will highlight how those
involved in supporting both older people and their unpaid carers can
contribute to optimising the benefits of transition and minimising the
more negative aspects of the experience.

  It should be remembered that not all older people move in old age,
and that for those who do move the motivations are varied and often
complex. At one end of the spectrum will be the individual remaining

in the home they have occupied for many years, perhaps accessing a modest amount of domiciliary support. At the other end of the spectrum a single individual may experience moves encompassing sheltered housing, extra-care housing and a care home, concluding perhaps with hospital-based palliative care. A concept often referred to in this context is the 'escalator of care'. Nonetheless, only 4% of the UK population aged 75 to 84 and 17% aged 85 and over currently live in a care home.

Ageing in place: accessing support

For those living in their own home, opening the door to some element of paid support indicates a transition, however modest, to a form of dependency on others. The privacy of an individual's own home is being invaded and, however positive the attitude towards receiving support, there will be a period of adjustment. Things may be done in a different way; traditional routines may be challenged; private places may have to become public. Compromise and trade-off may often occur. Individuals who may be receiving support for a limited period, for example during a period of reablement, may value the intervention but express relief when it is over and they can regain their own territory.

Transitions in place with associated loss of independence become most evident when individuals are receiving higher levels of support. Curtice et al (2002) explored the experiences of 150 individuals and their unpaid carers receiving intensive domiciliary support in three areas in Scotland. The mean paid weekly care hours was 31, and over 60% remained in their own homes nine months after the initial interview. These were individuals who might otherwise be at risk of entering institutional care: many had expressed a determination to remain at home, which had led to more intensive support packages. Eighty-five per cent had never considered moving: home was important for the location, for the fabric of the house and for the accumulated memories. Privacy and security were also important. Many older people and their carers identified common features they were looking for in the provision of support, for some in contrast to what they were experiencing:

- a small team of regular care workers;
- flexibility in the tasks that could be performed by care workers;
- monitoring of the care plan – training of all staff in the needs of the individual;

- one trusted individual within the care network who could advocate for the person's needs;
- the opportunity to engage in more preventive elements of support.

A particular challenge for these more intensive models of support, shared also with situations of ongoing nursing and palliative support, is the extent to which the domestic home may be transformed into more of a care setting. Hoists, placing a bed in the living room, the need for a commode, the visibility of drips, syringe drivers or other equipment may all militate against a homely setting. Such challenge is not just physical; one anecdote relates to the son of a mother receiving augmented home care. He used to drop in on his mother every morning to bring her the newspaper on his way to work. Encountering two support workers busy getting his mother washed and fed, he stopped calling by. Fortunately in this instance the care workers recognised the dilemma and adjusted their timing accordingly so that the son resumed his morning visit. Similar tensions have been reported by co-resident carers, no longer at ease in their own home. Indeed, it can be argued that more intensive models of domiciliary support, including night-time visits, may be easier to achieve for those living on their own.

Interestingly, Curtice et al (2002) also interviewed 63 individuals recently admitted to care homes within the same local authority areas. Many considered that there had been a lack of choice, and over half expressed a preference for their own home. Only a minority had made a positive choice of institutional care. Few had had a care plan while in their own home and levels of domiciliary support had been low; two thirds had not been offered any additional support at home prior to admission. The physical and total dependency levels of those admitted to care homes were significantly lower than for those receiving the intensive support at home, while mental dependency levels were similar. This study highlights the complexity of this arena; it is not a simple pattern of transitions along a continuum of dependency.

Entering a care home

Making the decision as to whether to move to institutional care has been described by Willcocks et al (1987, p 134) as 'alien, different and distanced from all other experiences which people accumulate over a lifetime'. Relocation epitomises many of the aspects of transition explored throughout this volume: unease and uncertainty in face of the unknown; individual capacity for adjustment; and resilience in response to discontinuities. Traditionally, negative portrayals of institutional care as the 'final sign of failure' or the 'place of last resort' have more recently been challenged. Reed and Payton (1996) and Oldman and Quilgars (1999) both emphasise the extent to which the experience of the individual is a complex mix of individual interpretation and negotiation of meaning in response to circumstances and events. For example, excessive constraint for one will be perceived as reassuring security for another. The lesson throughout is one of supporting individual needs, preferences and choices.

In respect of the move to a care home, an early formulation of key parameters by Chenitz (1983) remains valid. He argued that the experience of moving to a care home is likely to be a product of the following factors:

- *centrality* – how much of the move is perceived to affect the older person's control over their life, especially in terms of maintaining a sense of independence and autonomy;
- *desirability* – the extent to which the move is perceived as being desirable and taken by choice;
- *legitimation* – whether there is a perceived legitimate reason for moving;
- *reversibility* – whether the move is considered to be permanent or temporary.

Nolan et al (1996) drew on this work in identifying the basic conditions that shape how an individual adjusts to their new environment. They argue, however, that positive options, of anticipation and embracing, should be added to reflect those who may be looking forward to the option or may see it as the preferred alternative. They suggest that four attributes of a transition predict whether it is regarded as a positive choice:

- *anticipation* – the extent to which prior thought and discussion has been given to placement;
- *participation* – the extent to which the older person and their carer(s) have participated fully in the decision-making process;
- *information* – the quality of information and advice;
- *exploration* – of alternatives to care, of a range of care homes, and of emotional responses to the prospect of placement.

Building on these elements and on a number of empirical studies, they suggest that a fourfold typology of admissions can be identified:

- *positive choice* – well informed and mostly desirable;
- *rationalised alternative* – the most frequent and indicating that individuals can give a coherent explanation for the move;
- *discredited option* – one in which expectations have been spoiled, for example the single room that was promised is not provided, or other residents are not able to communicate, or a stay that was offered as temporary is proving to be permanent;
- *fait accompli* – the worst case scenario, for example a crisis admission without choice.

The process of adjusting to living in a care home has been explored by a number of authors, who highlight features such as the loss of identity, the lowering of self-esteem and the reduced sense of personhood. Reed et al (1998a) focused on the process of adjustment to the new physical and social environment – the 'complex negotiation of their new social world' (p 157). They identified a process that they term 'constructing familiarity', new entrants building on sparse information as a means of breaking the ice and making contact with existing residents. An individual may, for example, amplify their knowledge of a common acquaintance in order to establish a basis for developing networks and supportive relationships. The same authors (Reed et al, 1998b) explored the particular importance of location and of a sense of place. This impacts both practically in terms of sustaining friendship networks and continuing to participate in social activities, and in contributing to individual identify through a sense of belonging and shared geography. The authors illustrated the need to be sensitive to the fine detail of location, for example allegiance to former villages within what may appear a uniform environment: 'If older people develop and maintain a sense of self through the medium of place, and place has been an important feature of their lives, then this suggests that relocation to another place is a serious matter' (Reed et al, 1998b, p 860).

A somewhat different aspect of the process of transition to a care home is the loss of citizenship and participation in deliberative democracy highlighted by Scourfield (2007). He illustrates ways in which the 'third age' is often presumed to speak for the 'fourth age' and argues that effective advocacy support must be deployed: 'it is a massive transition in life. It is therefore important that, whatever other losses the person is experiencing, they do not lose the basic right to citizenship' (2007, p 1149).

Wilson (1997) interviewed 15 adults ranging in age from 76 to 97 who were admitted to one of three nursing homes in Midwestern USA. He identified three phases that individuals went through. Initially they felt overwhelmed, reacting emotionally to the admission with tears, feelings of loneliness and sadness, and a longing to go home. Particular problems included experiencing too many changes at once, having to adjust to having less personal space, and the reduction in privacy. Nonetheless, individuals made conscious efforts to hide their feelings, concerned to protect their families. This initial period was followed by an adjustment phase, where individuals internalised their admission and began to think about the future and everyday routines. Individuals tried to develop a positive attitude, to make new friendships, and to come to terms with the regulations of the nursing home and the reduced opportunities to participate in decision making. In the third, initial acceptance phase, residents began to feel more self-confident, beginning to take control of the situation, to get more involved and to look to the future. Those who had planned their admission progressed through the three phases more rapidly than those for whom the admission had been unplanned.

A systematic review by Lee et al (2002) summarises the range of experiences pre and post placement. They suggested that the feelings of loss and suffering that individuals experience can be grouped into three types: abstract, material and social. The abstract covers loss of role, of lifestyle, of freedom and, particularly important, of autonomy and privacy. Material losses include the loss of home and personal belongings, but the significance is not so much in the objects themselves, rather in what they symbolise in terms of the memories they evoke. Likewise, for many, home is associated with security, with control and with personal identity. Wherever possible, individuals must be supported to retain the symbolic objects they most value. Finally, the social loss is of family, of friends and, for many a key consideration, of pets. At the same time, however, there may be positive aspects to a move. A sense of relief and security may come for some from the knowledge that they will no longer be alone, or have the challenges of meal preparation, managing a household and getting out in winter. A feeling of safety is key for many.

Lee et al (2002) suggested a sequence of experiences in dealing with placement. Initially there may be passive acceptance: individuals confirm, fit in, go along with what is expected and accept the rules and norms. A second stage may be making the best of available choices, focusing on the aspects of life that can be controlled, for example controlling when they go to bed or stocking up on favourite foods. Later still, individuals may reframe their experiences, comparing themselves with others in the care home and convincing themselves that they are not useless. The presence of others with greater disabilities may help individuals to put their experience in perspective and help them cope with the transition. Such framing does, however, require a degree of cognition that may no longer be available to many of those now admitted to the care home environment. Lee et al cite an earlier study by Brooke that, following interviews with individuals moving to a nursing home, suggested a timeframe of disorganisation during the first two months, reorganisation during the third, relationship building during the third and fourth and stabilisation over months four to six.

It should, however, be remembered that a number of individuals will experience further transitions *between* care homes. In the study by Reed et al (1998a) cited above, 13 of 44 residents had moved within the 12-month follow-up period. The pattern of moves was varied: five from residential to nursing; two from nursing to residential; three from residential to their own home; two from residential to other residential; and one from nursing to accommodation for the elderly mentally infirm.

In a further study, Reed et al (2003) explored with staff and residents in care homes in two areas the explanations for individual moves to another care home. They identified four different types of relocations. They termed these:

- *preference relocations* – moves where residents report that they have exercised choice;
- *strategic relocations* – moves where residents seek to pre-empt changes, for example where they hear that their current home is closing;
- *reluctant relocations* – moves that residents resist or disagree with, often where there are different perceptions of needs and providers consider that they can no longer meet the individuals' needs;
- *passive relocations* – moves described by the residents as arising from decisions by others about the level and type of support required, which they had not questioned.

An example of the last of these was highlighted by a family member: 'she didn't ask to come here, it was all arranged that she came here, she was never asked' (Reed et al, 2003, p 236). The authors suggested that decisions can be viewed as lying on a continuum; at one end the older person makes the judgement and takes the decision, at the other the views of others dominate. Williams et al (2007) discussed the role of the care manager in the situation when residents have no choice but to relocate on account of their care home being closed. The impact of such closure on residents' health and well-being is likely to be influenced by the way in which the closure and the move are handled. There is a likely but uncertain relationship between closure and mortality.

The importance of constructing a more positive environment for the transition to care home was recognised by Nolan et al (2006) in their promotion of the application of what they term the 'Senses Framework'. The development of the framework was prompted by a concern that the promotion of the concept of 'successful ageing', implying the avoidance of disease and disability, high levels of physical and cognitive functioning and active engagement with life, could lead to exclusion for the many in care homes who could in these terms be considered 'unsuccessful'. There was also a concern that the original intent of person-centred care had been lost and that the importance of reciprocity was in danger of being neglected: 'we believe the focus on individuality and autonomy that defines currently prevalent notions of PCC [patient-centred care] will further marginalise those living and working in care homes' (Nolan et al, 2006, p 6). A move towards a relationship-centred approach and a new philosophy of care seeks to capture the subjective aspects of care that should be experienced by all those involved, whether resident, care worker or relative. The six senses that were identified are:

- *a sense of security* – to feel safe and receive or deliver competent and sensitive care;
- *a sense of continuity* – recognition of biography, using the past to make sense of the present, and help to plan the future; working within a consistent team using an agreed philosophy of care;
- *a sense of belonging* – having opportunities to form meaningful relationships and to feel part of the community of the home, whether as a resident or staff member;
- *a sense of purpose* – to have opportunities to engage in purposeful activity, or to have a clear set of goals to aim for;
- *a sense of fulfilment* – to achieve meaningful or valued goals and to feel satisfied with one's efforts;
- *a sense of significance* – to feel that you, and what you do, matter, and that you are valued as a person of worth.

Such a strategy, Reed et al argued, should create an 'enriched environment' of care.

This framework has been adopted in the excellent work on quality of life in care homes being promoted by the My Home Life Project (Owen and the National Care Homes Research and Development Forum, 2006) initiated by Help the Aged. This seeks to promote care homes as a positive option for older people, celebrate existing best practice and improve quality of life through the development of a range of resources and practice initiatives. This is a UK–wide initiative with a specific arm, My Home Life – Scotland. Following a comprehensive review of the literature, collectively assembled from contributors throughout the UK (National Care Homes Research and Development Forum, 2007), eight best practice themes have been identified:

- managing transitions
- maintaining identity
- creating communities
- sharing decision making
- improving health and healthcare
- supporting end-of-life care
- keeping the workforce fit for purpose
- promoting a positive culture.

For each theme, a bulletin for care home staff and a research briefing is being produced. For the theme of managing transitions, the project's 10 top tips are as follows:

- a positive choice
- a trial run
- feeling in control
- providing information
- minimising pressure
- family members as partners in care
- getting other residents to help
- continuing with life
- a proper welcome
- supporting people through upheaval (Owen and the National Care Homes Research and Development Forum, 2006).

Impact on family members

Relatively little attention has been given to the impact on relatives of an individual moving into a care home; more often they may be subject to unfounded speculation on the ulterior motives for encouraging a care placement. Davies and Nolan (2003, 2004) conducted 37 interviews involving 48 people who had assisted with the nursing home placement of a relative. For 29 of the families, the admission had followed a hospital stay. The accounts of the relatives referred to the decision making in respect of entry to the nursing home in terms of 'making the best of it'. Three main approaches to the decision could be identified. For all, there were two main concerns: making the right decision about the need for long-term care and choosing the best available care home. For a minority (three families), there was a positive sense of 'making the decision' in a gradual and planned way, proactive rather than reactive. For a second group, the process was more one of 'reaching the decision' following a period of indecision; while the third group described a process of 'realising the inevitable'.

Whichever the experience, the experiences varied along a continuum on five key elements:

- operating under pressure or not
- in the know or working in the dark
- working together or working apart
- in control of events or not
- supported or unsupported, both practically and emotionally.

The authors also referred to the four transition attributes associated with positive choice identified by Nolan et al (1996) and discussed above in respect of the older person themselves. For relatives, the most positive experiences occurred when the admission was anticipated and there was an early opportunity to consider options. Few, however, had anticipated admission; moreover, over half of relatives had to take responsibility for the decision as a result of the cognitive impairment of the older person. There was a lack of support and of information and few opportunities to discuss their own feelings or to explore alternatives.

A number of practical strategies can be identified. These include ensuring that comprehensive information is available, including inspection reports, details of Commission for Social Care Inspection star ratings, and opportunities to spend time in the care home before the final decision. Health and social care practitioners should seek to work in partnership with both the older person and their family members, and should be sensitive to the pressures likely to be experienced by relatives and support them as necessary. They should ensure that the older person and their relatives maintain control over the decision-making process, avoiding dominance of professional opinions and mediating if necessary if the older person and their informal carer(s) have differing perspectives.

Wright (2000) interviewed 61 relatives (27 spouses and 34 children) of residents admitted to 35 independent sector care homes in the preceding three years. Five discrete roles were identified:

- *checking the quality of care* – this revealed particular concerns about inadequate stimulation, inadequate cleanliness, lack of respect for their relative's dignity, and drug regimes – inadequate information and excessive sedation;
- *companionship* – this was a key role but few had, for example, the opportunity to eat meals with their spouse or parent;
- *assisting with personal care* – however, individuals reported being told off by staff for cutting nails or helping their spouse to undress for bed;
- *handling the relative's finances*;
- *giving the relative practical help.*

Although one third of offspring felt that their relationship with their parent had improved since admission, most spouses felt that their relationship with their husband/wife had deteriorated. The lack of privacy often meant that visits could be difficult, and those who wanted to continue giving practical support were discouraged by staff. Relatives often felt disempowered. Considerable improvements could be achieved through encouraging care home managers and staff to adopt relative-friendly policies that enable them to retain active involvement and engagement with the person resident in the care home. Alzheimer Scotland – Action on Dementia (2005) has produced suggestions for relatives on how they can best manage contact with and participation in a care home.

Retirement communities and extra-care housing

Recent years have witnessed the development of alternative housing, with support options designed to meet the preference of the majority of older people to maximise independence in their living arrangements. A number of retirement communities and a range of extra-care housing arrangements have been developed, offering various options on funding, on support arrangements and on tenure. The aim of many of these developments is to minimise the disruption occasioned by the transition to more supported living and to maximise the potential for maintaining an active and independent lifestyle.

Although a range of models have been developed (Croucher et al, 2006), most can be defined in a typology that includes the housing and support-provider relationships, the scale and facilities of the buildings, the allocation policy and the tenure options. A key element is that people have their own self-contained homes and a legal right to occupy the property. The home can be owned, rented, leasehold, or part owned and part rented. Often, however, it is the philosophy surrounding the development, over and above these dimensions, which provides the defining ethos. In addition, developments may include a care home within the site, recognising that a transition to more intensive support may be necessary, but seeking to minimise the disruption of the move. Alternatively, schemes may strive to support people within their own accommodation until death, the aim, for example, of the ExtraCare Charitable Trust.

It could be anticipated that individuals take the decision to move to housing with support for a variety of push and pull factors. The Personal Social Services Research Unit (PSSRU) is conducting an extensive evaluation of the first round of the Department of Health's Extra Care Housing Initiative, which provided funding of £87 million towards 22 new-build schemes to open between 2006 and 2008. The *Initial report* from Darton et al (2008) includes a discussion of the factors influencing the decision to move to an extra-care scheme. For the majority of the 417 residents interviewed, the decision both to move and where to move to had been theirs. Most had visited the scheme in advance, but less than a quarter had considered alternative options. For the residents with care needs, the triggers for the move had been their physical health, the lack of support services, difficulty in coping with daily tasks, and problems with getting around the house. For those without care needs, the key factors in their decision were problems in maintaining their gardens and fear of crime.

The factors that attracted individuals to the extra-care schemes included the tenant rights and the associated element of 'having your own front door', an accessible bathroom and living arrangements, the size of the accommodation, the security of schemes and the care support provided on site. The authors suggested that people were motivated by attraction to features of the schemes rather than dissatisfied with their previous homes. Although some had support needs, the majority were relatively healthy and moving in anticipation of greater needs in the future. Just over half of the residents expected an improved social life, while one third did not anticipate any change. It did not appear that the provision of social and communal facilities was a major factor in the move. The majority of residents expected to live in the schemes for as long as they wished, with a third having no intention of moving on. In terms of the move itself, two thirds reported that they found it 'quite' or 'very' stressful, the levels of stress higher among those without care needs. Of this group, 16% found the move 'not at all' stressful, compared with 39% of those with care needs. Nine out of 10 described their move as well organised. Two thirds of residents expected to retain a similar level of contact with family members.

The importance of the transition process is reflected in earlier evidence from Oldman (2000) – that residents were more satisfied in their new location if the move had been positive and one over which they had control. The minority of people who had been opposed to the move had not settled well into their new location.

For an individual scheme – Hartrigg Oaks – a detailed analysis is available of the reasons influencing the initial residents (Croucher et al, 2003). Key factors were not wishing to put pressure on their family to look after them, mentioned by over 50% of residents, and wishing to remain independent (approaching 70% of residents). As above, there was reference to the garden or home having become too much. People also anticipated increasing dependency or isolation – 'I had a vision of myself as an elderly lady who couldn't go out, sitting and waiting for someone to come and dress me and feed me, and I didn't like the idea at all' (2003, p 6). The authors suggested that unlike earlier studies of sheltered housing where people moved as a result of a deterioration in health, people were moving to Hartrigg Oaks on the basis of what they termed 'preparatory moves'. There were also a number of factors exerting a major pull towards the development, led by the quality of the bungalows comprising the development and the extensive care services (including a care home) available on site. York and the Joseph Rowntree name were also attractions, as were the flat-rate fees offered by the financial model. Half of the residents were attracted by being with 'like-minded' people and the amenities on offer were also a positive factor. As might be expected, there were some variations between different age groups. Those over 80 tended to emphasis the care services; those under 70 the amenities, social activities and location. Those not living with partners were more likely to mention the attraction of social activities.

A number of studies (for example, Bernard et al, 2004; Croucher et al, 2006, 2007; Evans and Vallelly, 2007) have examined the extent to which the aspirations for housing with care of independence, social integration and provision for a range of support needs have been achieved by current developments. Drawing on a number of studies, Croucher et al (2006) concluded that developments providing housing with care do appear to provide the independence combined with security that residents seek and that individuals express high levels of satisfaction. There could, however, be different understandings and perceptions of key elements such as independence.

As yet the evidence in relation to reducing social isolation is considered to be more ambivalent, with increasing frailty and the development of dementia leading to marginalisation and even some hostility. This emerged as a concern in the study of Hartrigg Oaks, the first continuing care retirement community in the UK. In the early days, the response to people with dementia provoked mixed reactions: 'one resident with early stage dementia sat alone in the coffee shop as no one would sit with her' (Croucher et al, 2003, p 53). Despite having a nursing home on site, individuals with advanced dementia were initially moved elsewhere. As the community has developed, however, it is felt that it has become more tolerant, individuals ageing together and seeking to support those who develop dementia to stay in their bungalow unit for as long as possible (personal communication). More generally, there is the question of whether housing with care can promote social integration. Early schemes tended to have different tenures physically separate, while more recent developments have sought to integrate a range of tenures without visible segregation. Evans (2009) demonstrated the impact of physical segregation of different tenures in a retirement village, epitomised in the title of the article: 'that lot up there and us down here'.

The social well-being of those living in housing with support is a key dimension. Evans and Vallelly (2007) reviewed the literature in this area and highlighted the importance of avoiding too simplistic an analysis. For example, social networks with family and with friends outwith the scheme may be more important than the less intimate relationships with fellow occupants. Moreover, some individuals prefer solitude rather than interaction with others around activities and such choice needs to be respected. Callaghan et al (2008) presentrf emerging themes on social well-being, a core element of the overall PSSRU evaluation, and again highlighted the complex interaction of a range of environmental, social and personal characteristics. For example, the balance between residents and staff in designing and leading activities varied across different schemes, as did the level of wider community interaction. The balance between 'fit' and 'frail' tenants can be an important factor. From their initial findings, Callaghan and colleagues concluded that the development of social life in a scheme is assisted by an active and involved residents' committee, interested residents, and residents able to bring existing skills and expertise into the scheme. Barriers to participation can include health and mobility problems, together with the timing of care visits. There is also likely to be a wide spread of ages, with potentially different tastes. As the evaluation of emerging extra-care schemes proceeds, more robust evidence will be accumulated on the impact of the detail of fabric and organisation on the quality of individuals' lives.

Supporting individuals with dementia

The potential of extra-care housing to continue to support individuals as dementia progresses has been alluded to above. Cox (2007) summarised the evidence then available, while Vallelly et al (2006) sought to evaluate the contribution that extra-care housing could make to the long-term care and support of people with dementia. Their study took the form of a three-year tracking study, exploring what happened to 103 people with dementia in 15 Housing 21 extra-care housing courts and looking in more depth at the experiences of individuals in six courts. Of the cases that ended during the course of the study, a 'home for life' was possible for about half of the tenants with dementia – 21 died and 22 moved to a residential or nursing home. Triggers for moving on identified by staff included repeated use of the emergency alarm system, distress, conflict and 'challenging behaviour'. There was little evidence of 'wandering' as a risk factor. Three elements of the extra-care environment emerged as particularly important in supporting independence: the freedom to some and go within and beyond the housing scheme; maximising opportunities to 'do things for themselves'; and having choice about how to spend their time. The authors of this study concluded that 'extra care with the right ingredients can offer older people with dementia both security and independence, and above all a good quality of life' (Vallelly et al, 2006, p 110). It is a preferred option for people with low to moderate levels of dementia.

A key discussion around extra-care housing is whether at a certain stage of dementia there should be further transition within the scheme to a degree of specialist provision. One of the courts in the study by Vallelly et al had a specialist dementia cluster and there was evidence that individuals were less likely to move on than those in integrated developments. Specialist care and support could be targeted at particular needs. On the other hand, however, there was less integration in social life and it could be hard for couples. As with other aspects of extra-care provision, further studies are necessary to establish a robust evidence base.

There is a more general debate as to whether housing with care and support can achieve its aspiration to provide a home for life, whether or not individuals develop dementia. Analysis of data for this study revealed that the average length of tenancy for those with dementia was just over two years overall (2.13 years), ranging from 1.91 years for those who moved on to other care settings and 2.36 years for those who died. This average of 2.13 years is almost as long as for those without significant cognitive impairment, suggesting that dementia alone does not have a negative impact on a person's potential to live independently in extra-care housing. At the same time, PSSRU research suggests that the average stay in residential care is not dissimilar, at 2.2 years.

End-of-life care

Most recently, Housing 21 and the National End of Life Care Programme have undertaken a six-month service improvement project focusing on personalisation for end-of-life care (Easterbrook and Vallelly, 2008). As part of the development of a 10-year National End of Life Care Strategy, the pilot project involved three Housing 21 schemes and focused on enabling individuals with terminal illness to die at home if this was their choice. Over the six-month period, it became more normal for staff to think and talk about end-of-life care; staff knew more about what signs to look for and how to respond; health, housing and social care staff wanted to talk about and plan how extra-care schemes could support end-of-life care; health professionals began to voluntarily offer additional support to staff in the housing developments; and extra-care staff knew more about local specialist services and how to access them. Four key issues emerged:

* promoting dignity and choice for the older person and for family carers;
* staff support and skills development;
* the links of extra-care housing to wider health and specialist resources;
* commissioning and funding.

Personal reluctances to speak of death and dying had often extended into the working situation, with individuals uncertain about what to do and fearful of doing something wrong. The importance of a shared understanding of individual roles in helping people achieve what they wanted was highlighted, together with the potential challenges where there was separate provision of housing and care. The project drew together a number of recommendations for achieving personalisation in end-of-life care.

The National End of Life Care Programme has published a key strategy on end-of-life care in England (DH, 2008a), arguing that how the dying are cared for is a 'litmus test for health and social care'. Half a million people die each year in England, two thirds over the age of 75, and the large majority after a period of chronic illness. Over half (58%) die in NHS hospitals, 18% at home, 17% in care homes, 4% in hospices and 3% elsewhere. A good death for many would include being treated as an individual with dignity and respect; being without pain and other symptoms; being in familiar surroundings; and being in the company of family and/or friends. The strategy is based on the best available research, on the experience of the hospices, on the National End of Life Care Programme (2004-07) and on programmes such as the Gold Standards Framework (GSF), the Liverpool Care Pathway for the Dying Patient (LCP), Preferred Priorities for Care (PPC) and the Marie Curie Delivering Choice Programme. It has been shown that training care home staff in the Gold Standards Framework can reduce the number of deaths in hospital by almost a half and reduce crisis admissions by over a third.

It is argued that a whole systems strategy is essential, with the care pathway approach both for commissioning services and for delivery of integrated care for the individual. The care pathway involves:

- identification of people approaching the end of life and initiating discussion about preferences for end-of-life care;
- care planning – assessing needs and preferences, agreeing a care plan to reflect these and reviewing these regularly;
- coordination of care;
- delivery of high-quality services in all locations;
- management of the last days of life;
- care after death;
- support for carers, both during a person's illness and after their death.

A number of key areas have been addressed by the strategy. These include:

- more open discussion of issues relating to death and dying, hopefully leading to a change in attitudes around death;
- attention to recording individual wishes, preferences and an agreed set of actions in a care plan that is available to all with legitimate access;
- development of a central coordination facility or locality-wide registers to ensure that people approaching the end of life receive coordinated care in line with their care plan across sectors and at all times.

The strategy was launched with commitment of £88 million for 2009-10 and £198 million for 2010-11. A number of targeted documents have also been produced, including one addressing end-of-life care in care homes (DH, 2006) and another focusing on information for commissioning end-of-life care (DH, 2008b).

For Wales, the Welsh Assembly has produced *Strategic directions for palliative care services in Wales* (WAG, 2003) and the *All Wales care pathway for the last days of life* (WAG, 2006). In Scotland, a national action plan *Living and dying well* (Scottish Government, 2008) has been published, addressing palliative and end-of-life care. This sets out five key areas with associated actions:

- assessment and review of palliative and end-of-life care needs – ensuring that all appropriate patients and carers are identified and their needs assessed;
- planning and delivery of care for patients with palliative and end-of-life care needs – implementing care plans for all patients and carers following a patient-centred planning process;
- communication and coordination – supporting individuals to participate fully in developing their care plan and making decisions; communicating across care settings and systems to ensure effective coordination of care;
- education, training and workforce development –ensuring that all health and social care professionals are equipped with the knowledge, skills, competence and confidence to care for the diversity of patients and families living with and dying from any advanced, progressive or incurable condition;
- implementation and future developments – ensuring that the aims of the action plan are met in a manner that is sustainable, compatible with quality improvement and patient experience programmes and based on recognised good practice (adapted from Scottish Government, 2008).

As highlighted above, one in five of the half a million deaths a year in the UK takes place in a care home. Badger et al (2009) address in particular the needs of individuals from black and minority ethnic groups who are resident in care homes and the extent to which their end-of-life care needs are understood and addressed. The need for monitoring both the numbers and experiences of these residents and their family carers is highlighted.

Conclusion

This chapter has highlighted just some of the transitions that older people may experience as they negotiate their living and support arrangements in older age. Key themes remain those of individualisation and support to the individual through the provision of information and advocacy to pursue preferred options. In respect of some of the emerging models of supported housing, however, there is a sobering reminder from the recent review by Croucher et al (2006) of the limitations of the existing evidence base. They list a range of key topics where 'currently the UK evidence base tells us little if nothing' about:

- how well different models of housing with care work for older people from different ethnic groups;
- quality of life in the specific context of housing with care;
- the role of 'telecare' and other assistive technologies – their usefulness and acceptability to residents, and impact on staffing requirements;
- gender roles and relationships in highly feminised environments;
- end-of-life care;
- who is best served in a housing with care environment – the fit and the frail, or just the frail?
- under what circumstances people should be expected to move on to different forms of care provision, and who decides.

Although it is essential that these issues are pursued, it would nonetheless be unrealistic to anticipate answers that will be definitive for all individuals and all circumstances. The challenge of managing transitions in the optimum way for the individual will remain.

Key practice points

- The meaning of home should be understood and the key attributes of 'home' should be available, whatever the location – security, control and identity. Individuals who move to care homes should be 'living in' rather than 'placed', making active choices, judgements and decisions.
- Opportunities to support people in their own homes through intensive domiciliary support should always be explored; communication should be developed to ensure that professionals, including general practitioners, are aware of current possibilities.

- Older people seeking support should be able to access detailed information on all the options available and should be offered practical and emotional assistance to reach a decision on their preferred option.
- The uncertainties and sense of loss around entry to a care home and the unease during the transition period for both the older person and their family carers and friends should be acknowledged.
- Particular care should be taken to ensure optimum settings and support for people with dementia.
- Training and practice shown to be effective in the End of Life Care Strategy should be widely adopted; unnecessary moves in the last few days and hours of life should be avoided.

References

Alzheimer Scotland – Action on Dementia (2005) *Letting go without giving up: Continuing to care for the person with dementia*, Edinburgh: Alzheimer Scotland – Action on Dementia.

Badger, F., Pumphrey, R., Clarke, L., Clifford, C., Gill, P., Greenfield, S. and Jackson, A.K. (2009) 'The role of ethnicity in end-of-life care in care homes for older people in the UK: a literature review', *Diversity in Health and Social Care*, vol 6, no 1, pp 23-9.

Bernard, M., Bartlam, B., Biggs, S. and Sim, J. (2004) *New lifestyles in old age: Health, identity and well-being in Berryhill Retirement Village*, Bristol: The Policy Press.

Callaghan, L., Netten, A., Darton, R., Bäumker, T. and Holder, J. (2008) *Social well-being in extra care housing: Emerging themes – Interim Report for the Joseph Rowntree Foundation*, PSSRU Discussion Paper 2524/2, Canterbury: PSSRU.

Chenitz, W.C. (1983) 'Entry to a nursing home as status passage: a theory to guide nursing practice', *Geriatric Nursing*, vol 14, pp 92-7.

Cox, S. (2007) *What can models of 'extra care' housing offer to older people with dementia?*, OutLine 6, Dartington: Research in Practice for Adults.

Croucher, K., Hicks, L. and Jackson, K. (2006) *Housing with care for later life: A literature review*, York: Joseph Rowntree Foundation.

Croucher, K., Pleace, N. and Bevan, M. (2003) *Living at Hartrigg Oaks: Residents' views of the UK's first continuing care retirement community*, York: Joseph Rowntree Foundation.

Croucher, K., Hicks, L., Bevan, M. and Sanderson, D. (2007) *Comparative evaluation of models of housing with care for later life*, York: Joseph Rowntree Foundation.

Curtice, L., McCormack, C., Petch, A. with Hallam, A. and Knapp, M. (2002) *Over the threshold? An exploration of intensive domiciliary support for older people*, Edinburgh: Scottish Executive Central Research Unit.

Darton, R., Bäumker, T., Callaghan, L., Holder, J., Netten, A. and Towers, A. (2008) *Evaluation of the Extra Care Housing Funding Initiative: Initial report,* PSSRU Discussion Paper No 2506/2, Canterbury: Personal Social Services Research Unit.

Davies, S. and Nolan, M. (2003) '"Making the best of things": relatives' experiences of decisions about care-home entry', *Ageing and Society*, vol 23, no 4, pp 429-50.

Davies, S. and Nolan, M. (2004) '"Making the move": relatives' experiences of the transition to a care home', *Health and Social Care in the Community*, vol 12, no 6, pp 517-26.

DH (Department of Health) (2006) *Introductory guide to end of life care in care homes*, London: DH.

DH (2008a) *End of Life Care Strategy: Promoting high quality care for all adults at the end of life*, London: DH.

DH (2008b) *Information for commissioning end of life care*, London: DH.

Easterbrook, L. and Vallelly, S. (2008) *'Is it that time already?' Extra care housing at the end of life: A policy-into-practice evaluation*, London: Housing 21.

Evans, S. (2009) '"That lot up there and us down here": social interaction and a sense of community in a mixed tenure UK retirement village', *Ageing and Society*, vol 29, no 2, pp 199-216.

Evans, S. and Vallelly, S. (2007) *Best practice in promoting social well-being in extra care housing: A literature review*, York: Joseph Rowntree Foundation.

Lee, D., Woo, J. and Mackenzie, A. (2002) 'A review of older people's experiences with residential care placement', *Journal of Advanced Nursing*, vol 37, no 1, pp 19-27.

National Care Homes Research and Development Forum (2007) *My home life: Quality of life in care homes – a review of literature*, London: Help the Aged.

Nolan, M., Davies, S. and Brown, J. (2006) 'Transitions in care homes: towards relationship-centred care using the "Senses" Framework', *Quality in Ageing*, vol 7, no 3, pp 5-14.

Nolan, M., Walker, G., Nolan, J., Williams, S., Poland, F., Curran, M. and Kent, B. (1996) 'Entry to care: positive choice or fait accompli? Developing a more proactive nursing response to the needs of older people and their carers', *Journal of Advanced Nursing*, vol 24, pp 265-74.

Oldman, C. (2000) *Blurring the boundaries: A fresh look at housing and care provision for older people*, Brighton: Pavilion Publishing in association with the Joseph Rowntree Foundation

Oldman, C. and Quilgars, D. (1999) 'The last resort? Revisiting ideas about older people's living arrangements', *Ageing and Society*, vol 19, pp 363-84.

Owen, T. and the National Care Homes Research and Development Forum (eds) (2006) *My home life: Quality of life in care homes*, London: Help the Aged.

Reed, J. and Payton, V. (1996) 'Constructing familiarity and managing self: ways of adapting to life in nursing and residential homes for older people', *Ageing and Society*, vol 16, no 5, pp 543-60.

Reed, J., Payton, V.R. and Bond, S. (1998a) 'Settling in and moving on: transience and older people in care homes', *Social Policy and Administration*, vol 32, no 2, pp 151-65.

Reed, J., Payton, V.R. and Bond, S. (1998b) 'The importance of place for older people moving into care homes', *Social Science and Medicine*, vol 46, no 7, pp 859-67.

Reed, J., Cook, G., Sullivan, A. and Burridge, C. (2003) 'Making a move: care-home residents' experiences of relocation', *Ageing and Society*, vol 23, no 2, pp 225-41.

Scottish Government (2008) *Living and dying well: A national action plan for palliative and end of life care in Scotland*, Edinburgh: Scottish Government.

Scourfield, P. (2007) 'Helping older people in residential care remain full citizens', *British Journal of Social Work*, vol 37, no 7, pp 1135-52.

Vallelly, S., Evans, S., Fear, T. and Means, R. (2006) *Opening doors to independence: A longitudinal study exploring the contribution of extra care housing to care and support of older people with dementia*, London: Housing 21 and The Housing Corporation.

WAG (Welsh Assembly Government) (2003) *Strategic directions for palliative care services in Wales*, Cardiff: WAG.

WAG (2006) *All Wales care pathway for the last days of life*, WHC(2006)30, Cardiff: WAG.

Willcocks, D., Peace, S. and Kellaher, L. (1987) *Private lives in public places*, London: Tavistock.

Williams, J., Netten, A. and Ware, P. (2007) 'Managing the care home closure process: care managers' experiences and views', *British Journal of Social Work*, vol 37, no 5, pp 909-24.

Wilson, S.A. (1997) 'The transition to nursing home life: a comparison of planned and unplanned admissions', *Journal of Advanced Nursing*, vol 26, pp 864-71.

Wright, F. (2000) 'The role of family care-givers for an older person resident in a care home', *British Journal of Social Work*, vol 30, no 3, pp 649-61.

NINE

From hospital to community

Alison Petch

Introduction

> Effective discharge planning is a highly skilled and difficult
> task, for it requires assessment, intervention, monitoring and
> evaluation to be completed in a very short time. (Rachman,
> 1993, p 111)

Hospital discharge is a common experience for many individuals in
the course of their lifetime. The circumstances can vary widely: from
the child with complex disabilities returning to the family home to
the older person of 90 years old returning home after a fall; from the
individual with mental health problems discharged after a lengthy
hospital stay to the individual with acquired brain injury following
a road traffic accident adjusting to a new way of living. Despite its
everyday occurrence, the challenges that arise around the transition
from hospital to community are some of the most intransigent in
health and social welfare. This chapter will seek to explore why this is
the case and to map out what can be done to improve the transition
back to the community for the range of individuals caught up in this
experience.

Exploring the evidence base

An early study conducted by Neill and Williams (1992) detailed a
common picture that has not yet been displaced. The focus was on
the discharge of older people (aged 75 plus) to home care in four local
authorities and included interviews with older people and carers and
with home carers at two and 12 weeks post discharge. Most of the
hospital admissions had been unplanned and the majority of the older
people lived alone or with another older person. One in five received
few visitors while in hospital and half the individuals did not have
relatives to assist with the return home. The result, as illustrated by

vignettes from the interviews, included individuals returning home to decaying food and unheated rooms. Delays in transport were common, with patients waiting from early morning until evening. Hospital car drivers did not usually see people indoors and some patients were left unable to negotiate steps to their front door.

Only for 8% of the individuals had the referral for home care been made prior to the day of discharge and for a further 18% on the day itself. Three quarters were therefore without immediate assistance and individuals could wait several weeks or even months for aids and adaptations. The predicted level of home care required at discharge was accurate for less than one third of the individuals and availability of bathing and chiropody services was poor. Over half of the older people reported at two weeks that they had felt weak or ill on the day of discharge and a quarter considered that they had been discharged too soon. Quality of life was not good and the responses of a third of those interviewed suggested possible clinical depression. At 12 weeks, most were severely disabled and housebound and two fifths were in pain. Home care had nonetheless been reduced from an average of four hours per week at discharge to two and a half hours. This research study was followed by workshops with health and social care practitioners to determine action that could improve the discharge process (Phillipson and Williams, 1995). Findings not dissimilar to those of Neill and Williams have been replicated across a range of studies in different locations and for different groups, although not surprisingly much of the focus has been on older people (Tierney et al, 1994; Victor et al, 2000).

Jones and Lester (1995) reported on a study in the south of Wales where postal questionnaires were completed by older people who had been discharged from hospital over the previous three months. Questionnaires were completed by 960 individuals; over a third did not recall any discussion of their discharge, and the majority considered that they had received inadequate notice – a third were informed on the day itself and a further 39% the evening before. Only in a very few instances (52) had hospital staff visited the patient's home to assess its suitability, and for some the resumption of services received prior to admission proved problematic.

A detailed study in two hospital trusts in the south of England (Clark et al, 1996) focused on 50 older people who had been assessed by hospital-based occupational therapists. This highlighted the tension between the desire to clear the acute bed as soon as possible and the time that might be required for adequate assessment and organisation of community-based support. Misjudgements at this stage can lead to a cycle of premature discharge and readmission. The discontinuity between hospital and community can also lead to occupational therapists (and others) being unaware of the outcomes following discharge and therefore unable to judge the effectiveness of their recommendations.

Further variation in the perspectives of different stakeholders in the discharge process – service users, carers and professionals – was highlighted in a study by Godfrey and Moore (1996) in six hospital wards in Leeds. Users and carers were often unaware of any assessment and planning process and carers in particular criticised the lack of communication. Problems already highlighted were echoed: long delays without explanation waiting for an ambulance; uncertainties around medication; equipment failing to materialise; and home care failing to visit:

> The first time my mother came home I'd arranged for people to put her to bed because she was a bit frightened. But they didn't come so she sat up all night. I rang home care the next day and they said they'd had a letter from the hospital to say she hadn't come home. (Godfrey and Mooore, 1996, p 60)

Hospital discharge was one of the key pieces of work undertaken by the innovative Fife Users' Panels, facilitated meetings of frail older people who would otherwise have little opportunity for a participatory role (Barnes and Bennett, 1998). Their proposals for good practice, based on extensive experience, were well received by hospital managers.

Carers' views specifically have been the focus of studies by Henwood (1998), Heaton et al (1999), and by Hill and Macgregor (2001) and Holzhausen (2001) for Carers UK. Almost three quarters (72%) of the 2,215 carers completing a questionnaire for the study by Holzhausen (2001) considered that their experience of the hospital discharge process was poor, and indeed appeared to have deteriorated since the earlier study by Henwood (1998). A particular feature was that carers felt they had no choice as to whether to take on responsibility for the individual when they were discharged and their own needs were often not assessed. Moreover, carers from minority ethnic groups, women and younger carers felt less satisfied and less involved with the process. Hill and Macgregor (2001) explored the extent to which the discharge policies of 23 acute trusts in the north-west of England considered the needs of carers. While there were often policies that stated the need to involve carers, there were few indications of practical suggestions or initiatives on how this should be achieved.

The discharge of individuals with mental health issues raises wider questions, with a distinction to be drawn between acute and long-stay beds. The resettlement to the community of individuals from long-stay psychiatric and learning disability beds has been widely addressed in the past (Petch, 1992; Emerson and Hatton, 1994) and is beyond the scope of this chapter. Moreover, much of the resettlement programme has now been achieved, with, for example, only a handful of long-stay learning disability beds still to be closed at the time of writing. Nonetheless, many of the issues can be considered common – the need for:

- active involvement of the person at the centre of the move;
- good communication and coordination across all parties involved in the resettlement process;
- realistic expectations in terms of timescales;
- attention to follow-up and review, acknowledging the likely need for reassessment once in the very different setting of the community.

A detailed study of discharge from acute psychiatric beds was conducted in Scotland by Simons et al (2002). This had two main phases, each addressing the main components of discharge policies:

- the admission process
- discharge planning
- interagency and multidisciplinary relationships
- the discharge event itself
- community support post discharge.

The first phase profiled policy and practice through interviews with 89 key informants across health boards, local authorities, health trusts and wards. The second looked at the outcomes for individuals from a representative eight health boards, with interviews at six weeks with 173 individuals discharged after at least a week but less than six months in acute psychiatric care. The Camberwell Assessment of Need was also completed by both the individual and the key worker. A second interview was conducted six months post discharge with 128 of the initial group. Fifty-eight family carers and 27 key workers were also interviewed. In addition, 65% of psychiatrists responded to a postal questionnaire.

Just over half of the psychiatrists (59%) were aware of any acute discharge policy and there was little evidence of active use of discharge protocols at ward level. Less than half the users and carers spoke of control and involvement in the decision to discharge them; carers also spoke of difficulties in gaining access to information and decision making. The notice given for discharge varied considerably, with one in five service users considering it insufficient. Just under a quarter of individuals with a psychotic illness and almost a third of those with a non-psychotic diagnosis could not recall receiving information about their medication; financial or accommodation issues were often not followed through; and arrangements for transport, provision of medication, emergency contact arrangements and final notification to community services were not always clearly communicated to other staff, users and carers. Overall, one in four users stated that they had had little support during the discharge process, while a similar proportion (29%) reported a mixed experience.

Consultants cited major difficulties involving community services in the discharge process, with half critical of the speed of response from social work and a quarter reporting problems in accessing community psychiatric nurses. There were also, however, examples of good practice, for example the use of mechanisms such as fax, video links and email to facilitate communication and the provision of personalised medication information following a campaign by the Highland Users Group (1996). The report suggested the need to identify ward-based discharge coordinators:

> A discharge co-ordinator should be identified to carry lead responsibility for all acute discharges within a designated area. This designated person would be responsible for screening all individuals on admission and identifying the smaller number for whom specific interventions around discharge are required. Wards from which individuals are discharged would be contacted on a daily basis. This would allow identification of new admissions who required to be screened and of individuals who were being discharged that day and for whom liaison requirements had been identified. The discharge co-ordinator would be responsible for creating continuity and co-ordination between hospital and community rather than the current disjuncture. The role of discharge co-ordinator would be specified as part of the wider workload of a specific individual; this individual would most likely be either a CPN [community psychiatric

nurse] or social worker with dedicated time built in on a
daily basis. (Simons et al, 2002, p 5)

For those requiring a range of inputs to sustain community placement,
an integrated care pathway should be developed, with the discharge
coordinator providing ready access to information on for example
diagnoses, medication, benefits, transport and community-based
resources.

Common issues

It will be evident that a number of consistent themes recur throughout
these studies. These common issues have been distilled in reviews by
both Marks (1994) and Taraborrelli et al (1998). They are also featured in
a series of reports from the Social Services Inspectorate and in a report
from the Accounts Commission (1999) in Scotland. It is indicative of
the enduring nature of many of these issues that, although these reviews
were published more than 10 years ago, many of the challenges remain.
These are summarised below.

Inadequate information

There are repeated accounts of professionals, service users and carers
all having insufficient information on various aspects of the discharge
process. Information on discharge policies and procedures is not widely
available on wards and for staff there may be various forms of 'custom
and practice', potentially different according to the individual consultant
involved. There may also be a wide gap between policies being produced
and their implementation at the frontline. It is perhaps symptomatic
that in the course of the study by Simons et al (2002) detailed above,
it emerged that the Chief Nursing Officer at the Scottish Office had
issued a letter in April 1999 to Trust Chief Executives specifying a
minimum dataset and standards for the provision of information to all
patients on discharge. The requirement was for these standards to be
in place across all clinical settings by the end of 1999. Yet, awareness of
this requirement among the respondents to this study appeared to be
minimal. For service users and family carers the challenge of accessing
key information may be even more difficult. Users often recalled the
somewhat Kafkaesque uncertainty as they struggled to make sense of
what was being planned.

Poor communication

Closely related to the availability of information, is its communication across relevant stakeholders, both within the hospital and between the hospital and community settings. There is a need for communication across a range of different professionals, patients/service users and with unpaid carers. Much of the detailed evidence suggests that inadequate communication bedevils the discharge process. Key information fails to reach social workers, community psychiatric nurses or general practitioners; staff fail to adequately consult the individuals most closely affected or to provide sufficient explanation of what is happening.

Inadequate assessment and planning

Despite much rhetoric that discharge planning should start prior to planned admissions or at admission for emergencies, there are consistent reports of inadequate identification of individuals' community and rehabilitation needs. Individuals have often not been asked about their home circumstances or whether they will be able to cope and, as vividly illustrated for example by Neill and Williams (1992), may return to situations they are ill equipped or too weak to handle.

Timing of discharge

The discharge process is characterised by competing pressures: the desire of the hospital base to free their beds as soon as possible, the request from the community base for adequate time to assess the individual and secure support services. Bed pressures may lead to precipitate discharge, exacerbating a more general complaint that individuals often receive inadequate notice of when discharge is taking place. The timing of consultants' rounds may not assist with optimum notice. There is also the phenomenon of the Friday discharge, a desire to minimise those retained over the weekend period.

Transport

The provision of hospital transport has been a recurring problem. Again, accounts abound of individuals ready early in the day, not least as their bed is required, but then waiting in a day room for much of the day, uncertain when and indeed if their transport will eventually arrive. For individuals who may be frail and already wary of how they

143

will cope on their return home, this extended wait can only heighten their anxiety.

Medication

Delays on the day of discharge – or even of longer duration – may also be due to delays in ordering, dispensing and distributing take-home medication. There may be little opportunity to practise self-medication in advance of discharge, and little provision of information about the medication.

Delays and inadequacies in the provision of community services

Perhaps one of the greatest challenges of the discharge process is that it requires complex coordination of different sets of services. Work on the ward has to be complemented by work in the community to assemble and ensure the timely delivery of general practitioner involvement, domiciliary support packages and perhaps access to day provision of various types. Management of this coordination may be particularly inadequate for those with specific needs, perhaps on account of learning disabilities or the need for assisted communication. Moreover, there may be ambiguities as to the level of post-discharge support that can be expected and delivered.

Reflecting on the complexity of the discharge process, it perhaps becomes less surprising that the problems have been so intractable. It is an arena beset by tensions. It epitomises the boundaries between hospital and community and between a range of different professional groups. It raises key issues on lead responsibilities and highlights the different philosophies and cultures of adjacent organisations (Glasby, 2004; Glasby et al, 2006; Henwood, 2006). In particular, as highlighted by Glasby (2003, p 43), it features as a 'major area of tension on the fault line between health and social care'.

The impact of hospital discharge on the patients and service users caught up in the process makes it essential that attempts to eliminate negative experiences continue to be made. Fisher and colleagues (2006) chose to use older people's views of hospital discharge as the focus for their exploration of using narrative synthesis in systematic reviews. The lack of participation in discharge planning was highlighted, together with the apprehension about discharge and the relationship between control over decision making, anxiety and other factors. They introduced the concept of a 'life planning framework', extending the focus beyond the event itself. This, it was suggested, would relieve some of the anxieties that hover around this transition: 'will I be allowed home?'; 'will I be safe or will I fall?'; 'how will I manage on my own?'; 'will I be a burden to others?'.

Policy responses

Over the years there has been a raft of policies seeking to address the transition from hospital to community. As early as 1963, *Discharge of patients from hospital and arrangements for after-care* was the focus of a circular from the Ministry of Health, while in 1989 a further Guidance Circular (HC(89)5/LAC(89)7) was issued in response to criticism from the House of Commons Select Committee on the Parliamentary Committee for Administration (DH, 1989). This highlighted three areas considered generic to effective discharge planning: a multidisciplinary approach, discharge planning to be started soon after admission, and involvement of patients and carers. At the same time, the Royal College of Psychiatrists (1989) produced its own *Guidelines for good practice in discharge and aftercare procedures*. In Scotland, meanwhile, the Scottish Office had issued a Circular on the Discharge of Patients from Mental Illness and Mental Handicap Hospitals in 1988, stressing the need for close co-operation and good working practices to be maintained between hospital-based workers and those in the community to ensure the smoothest possible transition from hospital care to the community (Social Work Services Group, 1988).

A brief, generic guide to good practice in hospital discharge was issued by the Scottish Office (1993) following the deliberations of a working group in 1993, while in 1994 a generic *Hospital discharge work book* was produced (DH, 1994). This sought to highlight practical issues for implementation by each of the key players in the discharge process. In 1995, new guidance (Circular HSG(95)8/LAC(95)5) replaced that of 1989, while in 1996, the Scottish Intercollegiate Guidelines Network (SIGN; SIGN, 1996) developed 'The Immediate Discharge Document', a proposal for a minimum dataset providing the information necessary prior to the final discharge summary. The key requirements for such a dataset were regarded as brevity, uniformity and versatility, and the proposed template comprised 21 main fields.

The importance of compliance with the SIGN guidelines was one of the features of discharge management highlighted by the Accounts Commission (1999) in its review of acute admissions and discharges. The Accounts Commission stressed in particular the need to ensure adequate arrangements for district and practice nurses to receive information on an appropriate timescale. It also sought to ensure the provision to patients of comprehensive written information at discharge, and detailed the elements for joint discharge agreements and protocols essential to interagency working. A particular feature identified by the Commission was the need to monitor discharge delays, with few trusts recording 'same day' delays caused, for example, by the need for transport or prescribed medication. Only a minority of healthcare trusts monitored the quality of discharge, and the Accounts Commission suggested that trusts should review their discharge policies to ensure that they clearly stated the underlying principles, set agreed timescales for action, and specified how the quality and efficiency of discharge planning would be monitored and maintained.

With the new century came renewed energy to tackle this apparently intransigent area, triggered in particular by concerns about the level and costs of delayed discharges. A key report from the House of Commons Select Committee on Health (2002) argued that delays in transfer should be seen both as a symptom and cause of poor hospital bed management, and as a failure of communication between health and social care. It also argued that it was important to focus on the experience of individual patients.

Part of the government response to the Select Committee report was to issue good practice guidance (DH, 2003), which updated and superseded the *Hospital discharge work book* (DH, 1994) outlined above. This 'best practice' workbook emphasises that discharge is a process rather than an isolated event, and that effective transitions are underpinned by a number of key principles:

- There should be a whole systems approach to assessment and the commission and delivery of services.
- The active participation of individuals and carers as equal partners should be encouraged.
- There should be planning from the earliest opportunity across primary, hospital and social care services.
- A named person should coordinate the process of discharge planning, responsible for coordination of all stages of the patient journey.
- Staff should work within a framework of an integrated multidisciplinary and multiagency team, working to manage all aspects of the discharge process.
- Transitional and intermediate care services should be used to allow appropriate use of acute hospital capacity and to achieve optimum individual outcomes.

- There should be an explanation of the continuum of health and social care services so that individuals are informed, understand their rights and are able to make informed decisions.

The three key elements for whole system working for effective hospital discharge are considered to be capacity planning, reviewing performance and hospital discharge policies, and interagency agreements. A toolkit was also produced to facilitate timely 'simple discharges (DH, 2004).

Policy and practice focused on delayed discharge

In recent years the challenges of transition between hospital and community have been epitomised in the spotlight focused on what over time has been variously termed 'blocked beds', 'delayed discharges' and 'delayed transfers of care'. A report from the National Audit Office (2003) identified a number of core factors contributing to delayed discharge:

- absence of alternatives to acute care;
- poorly coordinated or tardy discharge planning;
- delays in starting or completing needs assessments;
- 'bottlenecks' in post-acute hospital care;
- delays in preparing packages of care due to funding and workforce constraints;
- poorly coordinated or tardy preparation for day of discharge;
- lack of capacity in post-acute care in all health, social services and independent sectors.

Three key perspectives are identified:

- whether National Health Service (NHS) acute hospitals are handling the discharge of older people efficiently
  - delays in initiating discharge planning
  - poor coordination between hospital staff during care
  - competing priorities for staff time
  - delays in carrying out assessments due to resource shortages and poor communication
  - delays in making drugs available to patients to take away
  - transport not available to take patients home
  - shortage of specialist staff

- whether the NHS and social care agencies are working well together
  - networks of organisations providing care are complicated
  - health and social care organisations can have differing goals and incompatible methods of working
  - sectors do not share resources to correct imbalances
- what is being done in health and social care to develop appropriate capacity in health and social care – delayed discharge because of a lack of capacity in post-hospital care
  - underdeveloped residential and nursing care capacity (or equivalent alternatives)
  - lack of funding for care packages
  - lack of intermediate care provision and service transparency.

Concern at the level of delayed discharges led in England to the introduction of a reimbursement scheme through the 2003 Community Care (Delayed Discharges) Act and associated (binding) guidance – HSC 2003/009: LAC(2003)21 *The Community Care (Delayed Discharges etc) Act 2003 Guidance.* The scheme was said to be modelled on that implemented in Sweden (Andersson and Karlberg, 2000), and required acute health trusts and local authorities to agree interagency discharge protocols. This was despite concerns expressed in the 2002 Health Select Committee Report on delayed discharges that such a system would be excessively complex, a disincentive to interagency working and unlikely to be successful in addressing the wide range of reasons for delay. Financial incentives (£50 million in 2003-04 and £100 million in 2004-05 and 2005-06) were made available to local authority social services to facilitate the development of new service capacity and facilitate patient transfers.

The guidance on the scheme details the procedures to be followed before an adult patient is discharged from an acute hospital bed. If it is considered that an individual is likely to need community care services when they leave hospital and if any delays are to be reimbursed, an initial 'section 2' notification has to be given to social services for assessment at least three days prior to discharge. The authority should also have been notified of the potential need at the admission stage, together where possible with an estimated date of discharge. A second, 'section 5', notification then has to be provided at least 24 hours in advance of the confirmed date of discharge, with this date being jointly agreed by the multidisciplinary team. If discharge is delayed beyond the confirmed date of discharge because the local authority fails either to complete the assessment and/or to provide a suitable care package, they must reimburse the NHS for each day's delay (provided this is three full days after the initial notification). The sum involved is £100 per day (£120 in London).

In Scotland, an alternative approach has been adopted. Since 2002, the 15 health boards have been required to work with the local authorities in their area to produce a Delayed Discharge Action Plan, an agreed joint plan to reduce the number of delayed discharges across all types of beds. Definitions are different, however, from those in England, with an agreement between the Scottish Executive, NHS boards and local authorities that discharge from hospital should take no longer than six weeks from the time that the patient is deemed fit for discharge. Measures are therefore focused on reducing delays of six weeks or more, with a particular emphasis on delivering effective care packages for the 300 people delayed for more than a year.

At the time of the introduction of the Delayed Discharge Action Plan in March 2002, it was estimated that over 2,000 individuals had discharges delayed beyond six weeks, leaving one in 10 NHS beds blocked. A number of incentives were introduced to facilitate the plans: 1,000 extra care packages within the first year, and an extra ringfenced £20 million for initiatives by local NHS/local authority partnerships to reduce delayed discharges. A quarter of the money was available immediately; the remaining was conditional on approval of the detailed action plan for each area. These joint action plans were expected to:

- help develop more community care services and support;
- utilise existing home care places where appropriate;
- bring into use extra NHS continuing care beds where care home capacity is limited;
- increase the rate of assessments by social work staff;
- provide more support at pre-admission and admission stages;
- develop stronger liaison between social work and NHS emergency services to lead off avoidable hospital admissions.

Although there were no penalties for individual delays, the Scottish Executive made it clear that there would be close monitoring of performance in each area and action if partnerships failed to perform. This could involve sending in high-level support teams ('hit squads') to drive through improvements or withdrawing the delayed discharge monies in future years if the funding was not spent on the intended purpose. A national delayed discharge learning network was created to share good practice on tackling delays. Hubbard et al (2004) offered a detailed perspective on these initial action plans, arguing the need for a whole system perspective.

From May 2006, a new directive was introduced in which care settings were categorised as either 'short stay' or 'non-short stay' specialties. For short stay specialties (for example 'general medicine') the time limit for assessment and arranging transfer of care was to be three days, with six weeks continuing to apply to non-short stay specialties (for example 'geriatric medicine'). The latest available statistics from the NHS Scotland Information Services Division for January 2009 show 79 individuals delayed over six weeks and a total of 492 delays. Numbers fluctuate as demonstrated by there being no delays over six weeks at April 2008 (interestingly this had been set as a specific target), and total delays of 425 in October 2007.

A number of studies have explored in some detail the impact of the reimbursement scheme (CSCI, 2004, 2005; McCoy et al, 2007; Baumann et al, 2007, 2008; Godfrey et al, 2008). McCoy et al (2007) conducted a survey across all English authorities, which suggested that, contrary to public perception, the NHS accounted for two thirds of bed delays. They also showed that 62% of authorities had made no payments, alternative 'carrot' approaches being adopted. Policies to address delayed transfers from acute beds have featured prominently in recent years, with much scrutiny of whether numbers are declining and of the impart of the introduction of reimbursement requirements. Swinkells and Mitchell (2009) focused on the perspectives of older people involved in the discharge process. Interviews were conducted with 23 people classified as delayed transfers of care in two NHS trusts in the south of England. The mean delay was 32 days and there was a wide spread of reasons for delay. Overall, a significant level of disillusionment with prolonged hospital stay was reported, together with disengagement from the discharge planning process. There were high levels of expressed anger, frustration and low mood, somewhat different from the normally high levels of satisfaction expressed by older people. Respondents often felt disempowered by factors such as ill-health, low mood, dependency, lack of information, and the intricacies of the discharge planning process. The authors concluded that the extent to which individuals are involved in the planning for their discharge still needs to be improved.

The study by Godfrey and colleagues is of particular interest in that it compared the response to delayed discharge at three sites in England (with reimbursement) with two sites in Scotland (without) (Godfrey et al, 2008; Godfrey and Townsend, 2009). Interviews were conducted with 56 strategic managers and with 132 operational staff and a range of statistics for both countries was examined in detail. This study was also particularly successful in accessing the views of older people and their carers experiencing delayed transfers of care, interviewing 67 older people and 40 informal carers. The interviews were with people delayed for more than six weeks and revealed the boredom, frustration and loss of confidence that people experienced. They spoke of a loss of control and of low mood, with few attempts to mitigate:

> I fulfilled all my goals that we set and so I'm hardly getting any therapy anymore and that has been the case for a number of weeks now.... They say that for me, walking around the ward is dangerous because of the obstacles. [Leaving hospital] is essential for mental health as well. They don't seem to concentrate very much on the mental side of being here. So you can imagine the rest of my day is very long. I'm very angry that I'm not in control and I'm liking it less and less. (Godfrey et al, 2008, p 82)

Those in England were rarely aware of the reimbursement policy per se but were conscious of bed pressures and sensed that staff were under pressure to move them on. They were also critical of the territoriality that they experienced:

> It seems to me to be very territorial, this is my province, this is their province and once you have passed it on, you then go to the next one. There does seem to be a lack of – now then to accuse everybody of being uncaring perhaps is not fair – but professionally, it seems to me that their minds have been switched to acting in a 'Right that's another one out of the way, another piece of paper that can be filled in....' (Godfrey et al, 2008, p 83)

> I know that it can be difficult for the nursing staff because they don't know what's going on outside the hospital. But I was waiting for three weeks to speak to a social care manager about getting discharged. They didn't know, I asked them why and they says we don't have the spaces. Now even if things don't change, which they didn't I still wanted to know but I kept on having to ask and I felt I was being a pest but I was really desperate to know. (Godfrey et al, 2008, p 84)

Carers also felt powerless and were concerned at frequent moves across between wards to cope with pressures on beds. They often felt they had to put up a fight on behalf of their relative:

> To tell you the truth I was shocked. At the time I was livid … I sat on the train coming home from work, the phone rang and they said 'your mum is coming home tomorrow morning'. With the situation as it was – Dad was in the same hospital – he had had a stroke and since then he is now in a home. So Mum was going back to an empty house, no partner there. (**G**odfrey et al, 2008, p87)

A number of individuals were moved off the acute wards to interim beds but these appeared more often to be warehousing rather than an opportunity for rehabilitation. The authors of the study themselves concluded:

> The patients in our sample represent core NHS service users. Many were very old and had chronic health conditions, many were frail and often in the last years of their lives. What is evident in many patients' stories is that decision-making on discharge is affected by an interplay of factors – personal preferences, needs and desires of users and carers that may also conflict, and different professional perceptions about how best to meet needs. These were played out in the context of system pressures, service capacity and discharge processes. And as already mentioned, the conception of 'patient-centred care' and 'choice' does not take account of this complexity and the current focus on addressing the system and capacity constraints make such rhetoric appear hollow. (Godfrey et al, 2008, p x)

The suggestion is that there is a tension between the system pressures to speed up throughput, 'spinning the carousel faster', and the promotion of a person-centred approach. Patient choice could also be used as a factor in some of the gaming and loopholes that emerged around the use of section 5 of the 2003 Community Care (Delayed Discharge) Act: if an offer is made and refused, the delay is non-reimbursable. More generally, factors other than the introduction of reimbursement appear to have contributed to a marked reduction in delayed discharges in both countries. In Scotland, the incentives and sticks have encouraged a shared responsibility, with the delivery mechanisms locally determined through the partnership agreements. In England, the more detailed specification of the mechanisms puts the onus on the local authority and there was evidence that the social worker could be targeted as the scapegoat for having failed to deliver within timescales. There was, however, even within three sites, wide variety in implementation, from close regard to procedures to the introduction of a partnership agreement with a joint investment plan that avoided the need for reimbursement. The authors concluded that what is required is a wider focus beyond the entry and exit points, recognising mainstream the impact of associated elements of the system: intermediate care and reablement; avoidance of emergency admission and readmission; community-based provision; and early supported discharge.

The Welsh Assembly commissioned an independent review of delayed transfers of care (Longley et al, 2008). This stressed the multifactorial nature of the problem and the need to rebalance the pattern of care, eliminating unnecessary admissions to hospital. The authors highlighted in particular the difficulties in working across professional, organisational and sectoral boundaries, and the lack of a coherent set of effective incentives to encourage local agencies to tackle difficult problems. A total of 46 recommendations were offered. These focus on:

- designing the balance of care and support for patients and carers;
- reducing delayed transfers from community hospitals;
- deflecting unnecessary acute hospital admissions;
- improving partnership working to achieve integrated care;
- shared information and communication technology to support shared care;
- pooling and alignment of budgets;
- personal planning;
- patient assessment;
- choice;
- patient advocacy;
- improving efficiency.

In terms of apportionment of costs, there was a firm recommendation not to adopt a reimbursement system.

Conclusion

The challenge around the transition from hospital to community is to negotiate administrative and structural boundaries in a way that ensures the delivery of seamless care. Moreover, a dual focus is necessary: a need for large-scale planning to develop effective systems but small-scale detail to ensure appropriate responses to the individual. A key feature is the need to approach the transition process from hospital to community within the much wider framework of which it is a part. This is the clear conclusion from both the systematic review of Fisher et al (2006) and the study of reimbursement by Godfrey et al (2008) as detailed above. Indeed, hospital discharge is one of the strongest candidates for implementation of the widely promoted whole systems approach.

Key practice points

- Discharge planning should begin as early as possible, ideally before admission, with multidisciplinary involvement in preparation of the discharge plan and identification of the professional with lead responsibility for coordination of the process for the individual.
- The discharge process should be seen within its wider context and in particular should not be constrained by boundaries between hospital and community or between different professional responsibilities.
- Pressures to avoid delayed transfers of care should never lead to inappropriate discharges and shunting of responsibilities between different agencies.
- The individual patient, and where appropriate family carers, should be centrally involved in discharge planning and should be kept up to date at all times with progress towards discharge.
- There should be effective communication of the discharge plan to all relevant agencies, for example notification of the date of discharge to the general practitioner, collaboration with housing adaptations or provision of equipment, coordination with home care for resumption of community-based services.
- A key worker should take responsibility for ensuring that everything is in place and the process goes smoothly on the day of discharge including, for example, medication, transport and community provision, follow-up arrangements. This should be assisted by a discharge checklist.

References

Accounts Commission (1999) *Managing hospital admissions and discharges*, Edinburgh: Accounts Commission.

Andersson, G. and Karlberg, I. (2000) 'Integrated care for the elderly: the background and effects of the reform of the Swedish care of the elderly', *International Journal of Integrated Care*, vol 1, pp 1-10.

Barnes, M. and Bennett, G. (1998) 'Frail bodies, courageous voices: older people influencing community care', *Health and Social Care in the Community*, vol 6, no 2, pp 102-11.

Baumann, M., Evans, S., Perkins, N., Curtis, L., Netten, A., Fernandez, J.-L. and Huxley, P. (2007) 'Organisation and features of hospital, intermediate care and social services in English sites with low rates of delayed discharge', *Health and Social Care in the Community*, vol 15, no 4, pp 292-305.

Baumann, M., Evans, S., Perkins, N., Curtis, L., Netten, A., Fernandez, J.-L. and Huxley, P. (2008) 'Implementing the reimbursement scheme – views of health and social care staff in six high performing sites', *Research, Policy and Planning*, vol 26, no 2, pp 101-12.

Clark, H., Dyer, H. and Hartman, L. (1996) *Going home: Older people leaving hospital*, Bristol: The Policy Press.

CSCI (Commission for Social Care Inspection) (2004) *Leaving hospital: The price of delays*, London: CSCI.

CSCI (2005) *Leaving hospital revisited*, London: CSCI.

DH (Department of Health) (1989) *Discharge of patients from hospital*, DH Circ HC (89)5, London: HMSO.

DH (1994) *Hospital discharge work book: A checklist for community based health and social services*, London: HMSO.

DH (2003) *Discharge from hospital: pathway, process and practice*, London: DH.

DH (2004) *Achieving timely 'simple' discharge from hospital: A toolkit for the multi-disciplinary team*, London: DH.

Emerson, E. and Hatton, C. (1994) *Moving out: The impact of relocation from hospital to community on the quality of life of people with learning disabilities*, London: HMSO.

Fisher, M., Qureshi, H., Hardyman, W. and Homewood, J. (2006) *Using qualitative research in systematic reviews: older people's views of hospital discharge*, London: SCIE.

Glasby, J. (2003) *Hospital discharge: Integrating health and social care*, Abingdon: Radcliffe Medical Press.

Glasby, J. (2004) 'Discharging responsibilities? Delayed hospital discharge and the health and social care divide', *Journal of Social Policy*, vol 33, no 4, pp 593-604.

Glasby, J., Littlechild, R. and Pryce, K. (2006) 'All dressed-up and nowhere to go? Delayed hospital discharges and older people', *Journal of Health Services Research and Policy*, vol 11, no 1, pp 52-8.

Godfrey, M. and Moore, J. (1996) *Hospital discharge: User, carer and professional perspectives*, Leeds: Nuffield Institute for Health Community Care Division.

Godfrey, M. and Townsend, J. (2009) 'Delayed hospital discharge in England and Scotland: a comparative study of policy and implementation', *Journal of Integrated Care*, vol 17, no 1, pp 26-36.

Godfrey, M., Townsend, J., Cornes, M., Donaghy, E., Hubbard, G. and Manthorpe, J. (2008) *Reimbursement in practice: The last piece of the jigsaw? A comparative study of delayed discharge in England and Scotland*, Stirling, Leeds and London: Universities of Stirling, Leeds and King's College, London.

Heaton, J., Arskey, H. and Sloper, P. (1999) 'Carers' experiences of hospital discharge and continuing care in the community', *Health and Social Care in the Community*, vol 7, pp 91-9.

Henwood, M. (1998) *Ignored and invisible: Carers' experience of the NHS*, London: Carers National Association.

Henwood, M. (2006) 'Effective partnership working: a case study of hospital discharge', *Health and Social Care in the Community*, vol 14, no 5, pp 400-07.

Highland Users Group (1996) *Medication: A report on the views of the Highland Users Group on medication prescribed for people with mental health problems and the information provided about it,* Inverness: Highland Users Group.

Hill, M. and Macgregor, G. (2001) *Health's forgotten partners? How carers are supported through hospital discharge*, London: Carers UK.

Holzhausen, E. (2001) *'You can take him home now': Carers' experiences of hospital discharge*, London: Carers National Association.

House of Commons Select Committee on Health (2002) *Delayed discharges* (third report), London: The Stationery Office.

Hubbard, G., Huby, G., Wyke, S. and Themessl-Huber, T. (2004) *Research review on tackling delayed discharge*, Edinburgh: Scottish Executive Social Research.

Jones, D. and Lester, C. (1995) 'Patients' opinions of hospital care and discharge', in G. Wilson (ed) *Community care: Asking the users*, London: Chapman and Hall.

Longley, M., Beddow, T., Bellamy, A., Davies, M., Griffiths, G., Magill, J., Scowcroft, A., Wallace, C. and Warner, M. (2008) *Independent review of delayed transfers of care in Wales*, Pontypridd: Welsh Institute for Health and Social Care, University of Glamorgan.

McCoy, D., Godden, S., Pollock, A.M. and Bianchessi, C. (2007) 'Carrot and sticks? The Community Care Act (2003) and the effect of financial incentives on delays in discharge from hospitals in England', *Journal of Public Health*, vol 29, no 3, pp 281-7.

Marks, L. (1994) *Seamless care or patchwork quilt? Discharging patients from acute hospital care*, London: King's Fund Institute.

National Audit Office (2003) *Ensuring the effective discharge of older patients from NHS acute hospitals*, London: The Stationery Office.

Neill, J. and Williams, J. (1992) *Leaving hospital: Older people and their discharge to community care*, London: HMSO.

Petch, A. (1992) *At home in the community*, Aldershot: Avebury.

Phillipson, J. and Williams, J. (1995) *Action on hospital discharge*, London: National Institute for Social Work.

Rachman, R. (1993) 'The role of social work in discharge planning', *Health and Social Care in the Community*, vol 1, no 2, pp 105-13.

Royal College of Psychiatrists (1989) *Guidelines for good medical practice in discharge and aftercare procedures,* Council Report No 8, London: Royal College of Psychiatrists.

Scottish Office (1993) *Discharge from hospitals: A guide to good practice*, Edinburgh: NHS in Scotland Management Executive.

SIGN (Scottish Intercollegiate Guidelines Network) (SIGN) (1996) *Interface between the hospital and the community: A minimum dataset recommended for use in Scotland,* Edinburgh: Royal College of Physicians.

Simons, L., Petch, A. and Caplan, R. (2002) *'Don't they call it seamless care?': A study of acute psychiatric discharge*, Edinburgh: Scottish Executive Social Research.

Social Work Services Group (1988) *Discharge of patients from mental illness and mental handicap hospitals*, Circular SW10/1988, London: HMSO.

Swinkells, A. and Mitchell, T. (2009) 'Delayed transfer from hospital to community settings: the older person's perspective', *Health and Social Care in the Community*, vol 17, no 1, pp 45-53.

Taraborrelli, P., Wood, F., Bloor, M., Pithouse, A. and Parry, O. (1998) *Hospital discharge for frail older people: A literature review with practice case studies*, Edinburgh: Scottish Office Central Research Unit.

Tierney, A.J., Macmillan, M.S., Worth, A. and King, C. (1994) 'Discharge of patients from hospital – current practice and perceptions of hospital and community staff in Scotland', *Health Bulletin*, vol 52, pp 479-91.

Victor, C., Healey, J., Thomas, A. and Sargeant, J. (2000) 'Older patients and delayed discharge from hospital', *Health and Social Care in the Community*, vol 8, pp 443-52.

TEN

Taking transitions forward

Alison Petch

The chapters in this volume have addressed transitions in a diverse range of contexts – and there are of course others that would have been equally appropriate to explore. Beresford (2004), for example, completed a research review for the Children's National Service Framework on young disabled people and transition. She considered both the transition from childhood to adulthood and from children's services to adult services, concluding that 'the process of transition from children's services to adult services, and from childhood to adulthood is more complex, extremely problematic and, in many cases, highly unsatisfactory' (Beresford, 2004, p 582). She painted a picture of young disabled people experiencing leaving school as a time of loneliness, with minimal contact with peers and few opportunities to enjoy positive activities or develop future skills. At the time of transition there is a reduction in services such as therapies, hospital treatments and other medical care, despite ongoing health problems. There is a lack of information on future options and opportunities and insufficient specialist staff. At the same time, there is a lack of involvement of the young person and their family in plannng for transition, with low expectations and limited aspirations. There is some evidence of what can make a difference: specialist services and skilled staff, multidisciplinary and multiagency working, an adequate system for communication, the use of peer mentors, and support for parents in adjusting to the changed relationship with their son or daughter. Fundamental needs to be the recognition that the transition is not from one service to another but to a new life stage. Moreover, chronological age associated with service delivery may have little relationship to individual needs.

Beresford's review is symptomatic of much of the work around transition. In line with many of the situations outlined in earlier chapters, more is written about the challenges and inadequacies around transition than about successful strategies and achievements. In particular, there is less evidence on effective interventions and a lack of studies on long-term outcomes as individuals move into adulthood. This links of course to a much greater awareness in recent years of the need to prioritise the outcomes for any individual of the support they may receive. Service intervention, whatever the focus of the transition, should be concerned to ensure a positive impact on one or more aspects of the individual's quality of life. Dean (2003), for example, has explored in detail the housing aspirations of young disabled people and how they might be achieved. This broad concern with outcomes, the achievement of successful transition, should be at the heart of future approaches to all types of transition.

Remaining for the moment with the transition for young people, the Commission for Social Care Inspection (CSCI, 2007) has looked in detail at transition planning for young people with complex needs. It identifies six key prerequisites for successful transition:

- There is commitment.
- Young people and families are fully involved in the process.
- There is effective strategic planning and commissioning.
- There is a multiagency approach, with good protocols, systems and processes.
- There is a coordinated, person-centred planning process.
- There is monitoring.

In order to achieve these key elements, the suggestion is that Directors of adults' and children's services should undertake joint appraisals of local arrangements and commissioning strategies to determine whether they are fit for purpose. At the same time, the government should coordinate the priorities of its departments and ensure that policies support joint work.

Reflecting much more broadly across the diverse areas that have been explored in this volume, a number of common threads can be highlighted. In their individual discussions of transition, each of the authors has highlighted key points for implementation by the practice community. It is notable, looking across these recommendations, that despite the disparate nature of the transitions, there are generic themes that recur, common needs that require similar responses. This final synthesis will draw together a number of these common elements. These can be equally relevant whether considering an older person moving from the family home to supported living or an unaccompanied minor seeking asylum.

Allowing time for transition

A number of the authors have stressed the need to develop opportunities that allow for gradual transition, providing time for adjustment and adaptation rather than the 'cliff edge' of precipitate change. This in turn implies the need to be able to provide support over an extended period if necessary, avoiding premature withdrawal of support according to a predetermined timescale.

Enabling individuals to access information as soon as required

A common theme throughout the chapters is the difficulties many encounter in finding out the options available to them. Individuals are searching for information and clarification, anxious to determine what the future might hold. Staff may often forget that knowledge that is commonplace in their daily routines is often not readily accessible to those most in need of it.

Supporting individuals to be involved in a meaningful way, leading, where appropriate, key decisions from an early stage

Enabling access to information is only the start of the transition. Once individuals become aware of potential routes and alternatives, they can start to consider their options and to select their preferred pathway. For many older people selecting supported living, there should be the presumption of different alternatives from which they can choose; for adults more generally, personal budgets should enhance the opportunities for individual choice and control. For young people seeking asylum, the options may be more uncertain and more constrained. Notwithstanding such constraints, the available opportunities for active involvement should be maximised. A sense of having control is key to successful transition.

Acknowledging the uniqueness of each individual and promoting their preferences; avoiding policy foreclosure

It is important that in any situation, time and space is given to explore a range of potential options. Personalisation and the development of self-directed support, for example, present opportunities and possibilities not even considered in years past. Likewise, professional support staff should resist any temptation to typecast individuals or to slot them into predictable pathways.

Making connections

Whether an individual with dementia moving to a specialist unit or a young person divorced from their birth country, the importance of maintaining memories and connections should be appreciated and facilitated. The meaning of 'home' and how its attributes of security and identity can be replicated in different settings are key to achieving a recognised quality of life.

Telling the stories

Time should be taken to tell both the stories that lead to successful outcomes and those that are more problematic. Both individuals in transition and professionals providing support can learn from such stories, the lessons in inspiration or the pitfalls and practices to avoid.

Experiences of transition can only be enhanced by successful achievement of many of the initiatives that are current more widely:

- closer integration between different professionals and different agencies;
- a focus on outcomes highlighted above;
- the development of relationship–centred support;
- the adoption of a holistic perspective;
- an understanding of the diversity of cultural needs.

In addition, however, there are a number of mechanisms that can be more directly targeted at elements of transition. Dedicated posts – whether coordinators of hospital discharge, key workers for young people seeking asylum or transition workers for young people – can provide the essential combination of practical knowledge with empathetic understanding. Moreover, opportunities for job shadowing, both within and between agencies, can provide the stimulus to think more creatively about how needs can be met and barriers overcome. The opening chapter in this volume outlined the different stages that can be seen as common to experiences of transition, together with the role of resilience in allowing an individual to weather the disruptions of transition. The challenge for the professional is to develop strategies that can boost where necessary this resilience and enable the individual, whatever the nature of their transition, to achieve a positive outcome.

References

Beresford, B. (2004) 'On the road to nowhere? Young disabled people and transition', *Child: Care, Health and Development*, vol 30, no 6, pp 581-7.

CSCI (Commission for Social Care Inspection) (2007) *Growing up matters: Better transition planning for young people with complex needs*, London: CSCI.

Dean, J. (2003) *Unaddressed: The housing aspirations of young disabled people in Scotland*, York: Joseph Rowntree Foundation.

Index